Kids, Cameras, and the Curriculum

Kids, Cameras, and the Curriculum

Focusing on Learning in the Primary Grades

Pat Barrett Dragan

HEINEMANN
Portsmouth, NH

Heinemann
361 Hanover Street
Portsmouth, NH 03801–3912
www.heinemann.com

Offices and agents throughout the world

Library of Congress Cataloging-in-Publication Data
Barrett Dragan, Patricia.
    Kids, cameras, and the curriculum: focusing on learning in the primary grades / Pat Barrett Dragan.
        p. cm.
    Includes bibliographical references.
    ISBN-13: 978-0-325-00954-4
    ISBN-10: 0-325-00954-6
    1. Teaching—Aids and devices. 2. Pictures in education. 3. Photography—Study and teaching (Primary). I. Title.
    LB1044.88.B37 2008
    372.133'52—dc22   2007044102

Editor: James Strickland
Production editor: Sonja S. Chapman
Cover design: Joni Doherty
Cover photograph: Sagar Lal and Nicéfero Alarcon, Grade 1, taken by Pat Barrett Dragan
Compositor: Tom Allen, Pear Graphic Design
Manufacturing: Steve Bernier

Printed in the United States of America on acid-free paper
12 11 10 09 08   VP   1 2 3 4 5

Especially for Sherry, for many sweet reasons.

Contents

Acknowledgments

Those whom I most wish to acknowledge for help with this book are probably the least aware of their contributions: the kindergarten through fifth-grade students at Martin Elementary School in South San Francisco, California. I particularly wish to thank my first graders and the fourth- and fifth-grade after-school enrichment group for their excitement and enthusiasm and their eagerness to take photos, experiment, and write about their work. These students shared a multitude of ideas with me, and their efforts and their stories made projects come to life in extraordinary ways.

Another student I especially wish to thank is Tomás Flores, now thirty-six years old, who loaned me a very special picture for this book: the photo-crayon-pen motorcycle collage he created in my first-grade class years ago.

I would like to honor—in memoriam—anthropologist John Collier Jr., who spoke to my education class at San Francisco State University when I was a student there and shared the idea of using photographs to see what was really going on in the classroom. Collier hailed the camera as "an eye with a memory" and believed that visual messages could be even more important than those expressed in words. I was fascinated with his ideas at the time and have worked to explore them ever since. I also want to thank his son, anthropologist Malcolm Collier, who collaborated with him on the second edition of his book *Visual Anthropology: Photography as a Research Method* (Collier, Collier, and Hall 1986). I appreciate his having contacted me to answer questions about his father and their work in this field.

I would like to thank Heinemann and the entire wonderful team who worked to help me bring this book to fruition, particularly Jim Strickland, my editor.

My former Heinemann editor and dear friend Lois Bridges, now with Scholastic, championed my book from the start and was crucial in helping shape it. Thank you, Lois, for the many ways you help me, and for the gift of believing in me as a writer. I also thank Don Graves, Stephen Cary, and Bob Sizoo for offering encouraging words when I most needed them.

I thank Philanthropic Ventures, Oakland, California for a small grant that helped with this project, and a donor who wishes to remain anonymous for generous financial assistance. Ramiro Orta, Apple computer trainer and professional photographer, was a great help to me with camera tips and ideas for teaching photography. And I wish to thank Phil Erskine, computer tech extraordinaire, who always comes to my rescue and did so yet again.

A big thank-you to my family for their incredible support, especially to my sister Sherry, who helped me in more ways than there are stars in the sky. I send a big thanks to my brother Jim and his wife, Debi, and to my wonderful mother, who wanted to help me and was always there to listen.

My nephew Mike, the soul of patience, helped me with technology, and my nephew Gabriel shared with me those exhilarating moments when he first got a camera in his hands. Tiana, Cathy, Michael, Dan, and Will, I appreciate your support as well. I also wish to thank my family in Scotland, especially Margaret, David, and Janis.

Very special friends were there for me to offer encouragement and to listen. Marsha Oviatt was a great sounding board and provided thoughtful feedback as well as connections in Antarctica—including the wonderful contact with Paul Nicklen, photographer for National Geographic. My students and I also appreciated her classroom visit and presentation, as well as the digital camera donated by Marsha and her husband, Nevin.

Dr. Bev Hock was a wonderful resource for me, as was Dr. John Becker. Dr. Ryan James of Budapest generously shared his own ESL program and his ideas for using photographs with English language learners. Caroll Webster helped with donations of children's books and magazines, and my colleague Sharon Hui Ng provided a much-needed translation of an old Chinese nursery rhyme. I also wish to thank Dick Sperisen, art coordinator emeritus from the San Mateo County Office of Education, who is an incredible source of ideas for the arts and curriculum. I always say that when you talk with Dick you get about fifty new ideas a minute. And I am grateful to fifth-grade teacher Jocelyn Berke, a Martin School colleague, who shared her biographical writing unit and other ideas with me. I admire Jocelyn both for her project and for her passion for teaching.

I'd also like to thank Mimi Macht for her support and enthusiasm, and colleagues Eileen Christopherson and Joan Murphy.

In the summer of 2005, Alpha Delta Kappa, the international honorary society for women educators, honored me with an International Excellence in Education Award and a monetary grant for me to use as I saw fit. The ADK grant helped provide both encouragement and the means to purchase camera and printing equipment as well as some photography books for my classroom. I am so very grateful to the sorority both for the award and for paving the way for me to stretch my knowledge and my teaching with a project that means a great deal to me.

I just cannot complete these acknowledgments without many quiet thank-yous and a gigantic tribute in memory of my sweet husband, George. He gave me constant and steadfast support along with deep wisdom and advice, all wrapped up in love and laughter. How he would have enjoyed this book!

Introduction

We don't see things as they are; we see them as we are.
—Anaïs Nin

"Wow; there are logs floating in the Bay," Gabe yelled in excitement. My nephew was looking through the camera lens with wonder, snapping photos of everything that caught his curious eye for detail. The eleven-year-old had never been on a boat before. For that matter, he hadn't used a camera before either. Both experiences thrilled him so much that he could hardly contain himself. As Gabriel focused his disposable camera on the waves behind the hydrofoil boat that was taking his family on a "tourist trip" to Alcatraz—the former federal prison built on twelve acres of rock on an island in San Francisco Bay—he asked, "What makes the water ripple like that behind the boat?" He also worried that a freighter headed for the San Francisco-Oakland Bay Bridge would never fit under its span. Predicting an imminent disaster, he shot several photos of the ship and marveled when the vessel *did* pass under the bridge—and that the disaster never occurred. It was a matter of learning how perspective works.

Most magical of all to Gabriel was the way the city of San Francisco would be visible, as we left the pier and sped away toward Alcatraz, only to repeatedly vanish and then reappear again and again as the fog lifted and returned. Gabe photographed a sequence of this vanishing act—moment to moment—snapped it up, recorded it on film. He learned about the changing nature of perception and reality.

Other sights fascinated him, including the guard tower and the lighthouse. As soon as we got off the boat, Gabriel knelt down and took a photo straight up the Alcatraz lighthouse, from base to top, capturing the distorted image, all the while asking questions about the structure: "How steep are the stairs inside? Do they curve? How many people can fit? What was it like to work there? Did guards ever sleep there? Are there bathrooms?"

Gabe's camera became an extension of his thoughts as he muttered, ran, exulted, and focused. He took pictures of things that caught his eye: things he wondered about and wanted to know. Ultimately, the photos would hold onto and record those specific moments so he could think about them and reflect on them later.

When they get a chance to take photographs, children in my first-grade class, as well as those from fourth and fifth grades in my after-school enrichment program, have reactions similar to Gabe's. Whether using disposable or digital cameras, my students are tremendously motivated to express themselves through the camera's eye, record what they see and want to remember, and experience the joys of independent thought and inquiry.

I have used photography and photo ideas in the classroom in many ways since the beginning of my teaching career. Sometimes my focus has been on incorporating photographs into the curriculum by melding writing and photos, using personal pictures to help children create original art and fantastic stories. I frequently use photographs as a tool to help me see details of what is going on in the classroom and to help me learn about social and cultural interactions between students. Photos are great tools to help me teach a variety of cross-curricular lessons. We record a lot of our learning photographically, especially on field trips and excursions. And I always count on photographic images to help children remember the place and the learning. In addition to the subject of the field trip, I photograph my students reading, making friends, and solving problems. Through the visual image, children learn about themselves, which, in an existential way, helps them to value themselves and to shape their lives. The photos, and children's reactions to them, help me learn about my students and what is important to them, which helps me teach.

I encourage kids to use cameras for inquiry, for celebrations, for making personal records, and for sharing, recording, and examining their lives. Using a camera as a tool gives students a "voice"—another way to communicate as they acquire language. I find teaching photographically to be especially rewarding when I work with English language learners. Through photos I can help these students make sense of their experiences and find a way to connect with those around them. Using cameras can be a compelling activity, especially for children who are struggling to express themselves. This year I've extended my use of photos to create games and lessons to develop children's vocabulary and conversational abilities, to learn about nouns and verbs and other parts of speech, to learn word wall and vocabulary words and to practice descriptive language. I use children's photographs on charts to illustrate teaching points and focus on sequence, comprehension, math and science concepts, and even directions, such as "How to Glue," "Remember to Stand Up for Yourself," and "Ways We Do Buddy Reading." Every area of the curriculum lends itself to photography-centered teaching.

Some giant projects have grown out of our photographic experiences. One of the best is the creation of Personal Memoirs: compilations of photographs and writing that become individual photograph albums. Another large undertaking that has evolved from our picture taking is our school newspaper. My students have been using photos and their own group-written text to create a one-page ledger-sized school periodical and publish it once a week. This is an astounding achievement with ramifications and learning across all curriculum areas. I'll share more about "Personal Memoirs" in Chapters 2 and 8, and "The Kids' Press" in Chapter 6.

Another favorite project has been to create group and individual stories, illustrated with my students' art and photographs, using a book called *Real ePublishing, Really Publishing! How to Create Digital Books by and for All Ages.* The excitement when we create a new book and admire and read it together is not to be believed! My favorite book creation of the year has been *Our Balloon Man*—the story of the day Hector's father came to school to make balloon animals and flowers with our class. Once I figured how to make this web book, using both online directions and the above-mentioned Heinemann publication by Mark W. F. Condon and Michael McGuffee, it was simple to make copies for each student. These small guided reading-sized booklets are easy to create and very motivational to read: They honor students' lives, celebrate their writing, art, and other interests, and further their reading abilities in giant increments. It is possible to make books in several different sizes using this program.

This year, my after-school enrichment class of intermediate students has produced a large photographic and writing project of their own—a literary magazine: *Special Days: Reflections on Things That Really Matter*—with essays written by the students and illustrated with their own photographs. This production highlights some poignant childhood moments. Students grew a great deal personally as their work developed. They are deservedly proud of the essays they wrote that resound with their own voices and the snapshots that illuminate their unique vision and showcase their stories. See Chapter 9 for more on this photojournalism project.

I am finding that just about everything I teach can be clarified, enhanced, and illuminated using cameras and photographs. Aside from photos taken at school by me and by my students, we make good use of snapshots brought from home: I duplicate and enlarge these photos on our school copy machine and make them available to the kids for their own use. I also use available images from the Internet to extend and augment lessons across the curriculum.

Although I prefer the digital camera for its flexibility, cameras of all types— digital, disposable, 35-millimeter, and Polaroid—are incredible resources in the classroom. They give students and teachers opportunities to view and use the visual image in a myriad of ways.

Camera Project Funding

Most of the ideas in *Kids, Cameras, and the Curriculum* may be done fairly inexpensively on a simple scale, while a few others may require a bit more monetary input. In Chapter 3 I will share some ideas for funding projects, as well as thoughts on keeping costs down. I will also include suggestions for types of equipment to purchase. Those of us in the classroom spend far too much of our own money to try new things and make exciting learning possible. It is important to get what we need and spend the least amount we can. I have to say that in the case of this project it has all been worth the expense, although I am always looking for ways to cut costs.

Using photos and cameras is the best way I have found to get to know my students and how they learn and to give kids impetus for creativity, personal growth, self-awareness, and self-expression. I can do this kind of teaching without time away from "the basics" I am required to teach. The skills developed through the camera project build up basic skills in exciting and personally relevant ways, all the while adhering to grade-level standards.

It's Not Your Equipment That's Important!

As photographer Ken Rockwell tells us in his web article, "Your Camera Does Not Matter" (2006), the important thing in photography isn't the equipment you use, but your ideas, your vision, the way you see. Ramiro Orta, a commercial photographer and a professional trainer at the Apple Computer store, feels photo results are 10 percent due to the camera, and 90 percent because of the expertise of the person who took the picture. "It's the eye that's important, not the camera," he says. Photographer Ernst Haas believes good photography is also about the rush you get when you capture the moment. When asked advice about the best wide-angle lens he said, "Two steps back and wait for the 'ah-ha.'"

Working together with cameras and photos my students and I get lots of "ah-ha's!"

Kids, Cameras, and the Curriculum is *not* meant to be a book about technology, which changes daily and can often be beyond our school and personal budgets, but a book of ideas on ways to simply and meaningfully connect kids and cameras and use photography to fuel learning. When we use the equipment and technology available to us, no matter how elemental, we can really take off! Success is a result of a way of seeing and is not dependent upon certain tools and materials. We just use what we have and let the process unfold!

In *Kids, Cameras, and the Curriculum* I want to share my photographic experiments, joys, and adventures with others like me who strive to create a child-centered classroom and who are fascinated by the power of reflective teaching and of the reflective lens.

1

Seeing the Classroom
Through the Camera's Eye

The more you see, the more you know,
And the more you know, the more you see.
—John Hitchcock, anthropologist

 When I was a graduate student pursuing an elementary teaching credential, a defining moment for me was attending a lecture by John Collier Jr., an anthropologist who taught on campus. I became fascinated with Collier's idea of using a camera in the classroom to learn more about my students by taking and studying classroom photos as a new way of seeing and analyzing information.

Only recently, years later, I learned that John Collier Jr. was instrumental in founding visual anthropology, a new branch of anthropology. His book on using photography and video to gain an understanding of human behavior, *Visual Anthropology: Photography as a Research Method* (Collier, Collier, and Hall 1986), has become a classic with everyone, not just anthropologists. *Visual Anthropology*, written and updated with his son, Malcolm Collier, also an anthropologist at San Francisco State University, details ways to take photos without making subjects feel uncomfortable and shows how to use these pictures to gather information and to study—ideas important for teachers.

I did, and still do, use my camera in the classroom to see the complete picture, an impossible feat while occupied with teaching. As Collier suggests, it is possible to see so much more when viewing a photograph of your class involved in an activity: the way children relate to each other, what is happening at that given moment, the children's body language, and how they feel about their learning, their teacher, and their classmates. There is information to be gleaned about the setting, such as items on tables and classroom walls. In the classroom, as well as in family pictures, placement of individuals can be telling. Is there a group member who stands somewhat distanced from others? Which members seem close and central to the photo? What does the image tell us about prestige and group standing? Who wields the power in this picture? Who commands attention? Is there anyone we cannot see well? Is there someone who is apt to be forgotten or overlooked? Are there students who have turned away or chosen not to show their faces? And are there those who want their faces right out in front, oblivious to the spatial needs of people around them?

While Collier advocates using videos and movies in addition to photos, I chose to focus on still photographs for the purposes of this book. It is worth noting, for teachers interested in videos, that many digital cameras have this capability, and camera support booklets contain step-by-step instructions for creating videos. This is a wonderful way to put together informative shows for parents, field trip records, and a multitude of lessons.

An important task I address right away in the school year, even before parent-teacher conferences, is to describe our photography project and ask parents for a signed permission form releasing me to take photographs of their child and use them in class displays and other curriculum projects.

It seems I have been using photos in the classroom for my entire teaching career. I use them in lessons to promote self-esteem, to help students succeed in the language acquisition and literacy goals I have set for them, and to achieve learning in other curriculum areas. I have developed multiple ways to extend the use of photos and integrate this learning with other curricula, which I detail in later chapters. One prime use of my own photographs has always been to learn about my students, as John Collier Jr. suggests. Through analyzing my snapshots, I can observe all kinds of things that inform me about my teaching as well. Some pictures are for my sole use and edification as I observe children in the classroom and on the playground. I make other photographs available to children to help them celebrate who they are and learn about themselves. And I use some photos to personalize our classroom and to make learning more fun and exciting. We surround ourselves with photos on our classroom walls. And with our class digital cameras or a couple of extra disposable cameras, my students and I "catch" kids being diligent, clever, successful learners, as well as good, caring people.

Visual Motivators

Photographs are a way to focus learning experiences and help children see themselves in a positive light. With the children's and their parents' prior permission, I take snapshots of them as they work at classroom (and personal) goals. I use some of these photos to make charts and bulletin boards. For example, many first graders come into class at the beginning of the year concerned that they need to learn to read or worried about how they can get better at reading and writing. When I photograph individual children reading, writing, using math manipulatives, or successfully modeling other learning, I put these photos up on a panel (a hanging piece of colored butcher paper), a mural (a horizontal piece of butcher paper affixed to a bulletin board), or a chart made from colored poster board or 24-by-36-inch manila paper. I add titles that reflect my learning goals. For example, a display of photos of each child with a book, "reading," taken early in the school year, may be labeled "We Are All Readers!" or "We Can Read Books!" Titles are more powerful if the words come from the kids themselves. As one of my students, Sabine, says, "Reading is for getting smart!"

Talking Our Way to Success

Children frequently want to talk about these photographic charts, murals, and displays. When this happens, I jot down their thoughts. Later, I type their words in large font on the computer and add their reflections to our photographic exhibit. Displaying the children's own ideas in their own words helps to cement learning, and it furthers the drive to succeed. Older students could take charge of these caption-writing projects and displays. It would be a great project for them. First graders need help to integrate photographs and writing in this way.

I want children to see themselves successfully *doing* the behaviors we are working on learning. As the old adage holds, seeing is believing; photographic visuals starring kids help children *believe* they are powerful, successful, and more than adequate for the learning tasks that face them. Not only are these displays beautiful, but they are constant reminders of how well we are learning, how well we are succeeding, how smart we are.

The Photograph as a Classroom Still Life

My first photographic revelation occurred as a brand-new teacher when I snapped and studied a picture of six children working collaboratively on a social studies art project. I had been concerned about the frequent unprovoked anger one child seemed to feel for another, but I wasn't sure of what I was seeing. Then I captured Mary Ann on film giving Andrew, the mixed-race boy next to her, a look of total hatred. He continued working away at his art project, oblivious to her attitude toward him. The photo verified my thoughts about the situation and clarified for me that there was indeed a problem here.

Knowledge gained through photographs, as indicated in the previous example, gives the teacher a jump-start in understanding students and helps educators figure out ways to problem solve. A small vignette of classroom life can be illuminating. Photos, especially those taken of a group or small cluster of students, are a noninvasive way to kid-watch. These snapshots are also a permanent time-stopping device: evidence to use as we think about things later. Photographs can be an unobtrusive way of gathering such information. If students seem bothered by my picture taking, I do not include them in other photos I take. Children stop being aware of the camera activity when we photograph often (even snapping away without film or with no intention of printing the digital photos we take), and then their typical behavior and demeanor are easier to capture.

Child Study

When we study children and learn as much as we can about them, we gain powerful information about their personalities and their learning styles. We get ideas about how to teach them well. By observing things children say and do, we find out what works for them. We can then modify our teaching and our curriculum accordingly.

As I watch my students work and grow, I keep anecdotal notes. Through careful observation of children, I try to keep up with and ahead of my kids' needs and provide their next steps to success. For example, when I watch Joel, a child who does not speak much English (and who entered school speaking only Spanish), I see that he is edging his way to confidence and competence by watching other children carefully and mimicking their behavior. During sustained silent reading time, students are tucked up with books to read. They have chosen their reading material, but I have made suggestions to be sure they have access to exciting fiction and nonfiction titles of varied reading and interest levels. I want my students to enjoy themselves as they practice their skills and feel the power of reading.

Joel has chosen a difficult book. As I observe him, he glances at the page, points to an occasional word, looks around frequently, and even gets up sporadically and goes to other tables to "help other kids." Children know I prefer that they not wander during this brief time period. Joel knows this too. As I approach his table, I bring a few additional books to add to the selections available. I suggest to Joel that he might enjoy reading one of these books. I remind him that he is getting good practice when he chooses a book he can read and thinks about what he is reading.

Joel picks out a book, and I read with him for a few minutes, helping him track with his finger. He can chime in with words he knows. He seems to feel more comfortable, and after a little while I move on to see what is going on with some other children. I do glance at him out of the corner of my eye to see how he is getting on. . . . Ah . . . I see that now Joel is reading. He is tracking his words. As I watch him for a while, I see that he even appears absorbed. As this brief period ends, I decide to document this moment for Joel, and I take a candid picture of him reading. We look at the photo together on the digital camera's LCD (liquid crystal display) screen, where we preview photos before printing them. We talk about ways Joel is making progress in his reading and what he likes about the story.

Joel and I decide it would be a good thing to put the photo up on the wall near him, along with his own words about how he felt and what he noticed when he was really enjoying a book, really reading.

As he glances at his photo and his large printed words, Joel grins, and his eyes light up. I feel good too. Joel has made a breakthrough, and now he has an anchor to look at when he needs to be reminded what it feels like when you help yourself learn. We all need confirmation of those moments when we shine. Cameras provide permanent remembrances.

This kind of child study, which can take just minutes, is a quick way for teachers to observe and record information on a child's way of thinking and learning and gain a deeper understanding of behavior, needs, and abilities. I use a binder with a section for each child and make brief dated notes. A photocopy of a relevant photograph may occasionally go in my records as well if I want to document behavior or refer to the photo to jog my thinking. The camera is a good tool for me, and teaching this way gives me a better understanding of my children in the classroom, as well as my own effectiveness as a teacher.

Getting Children Involved in the Picture-Taking Process

As I became more involved in my photography project, I realized that I didn't need to be the only one taking pictures: children could take an active role in using the cameras themselves. I wanted to involve my students in their own learning using personal photos and even some pictures *they* thought about and chose to take. Using cameras with children this way has been the heart of my camera-study work in recent years.

By getting cameras into children's hands, I explore ways children look at the world and shape their lives, and I give them the opportunity to take ownership as they create photo and writing albums, collages, and other personal photographic artifacts.

My first graders really take to photography! Students love learning this way and enjoy sharing their projects with classroom visitors as well as their families. The class big books and other charts in print that they create provide reading materials they can't wait to explore. And our school newspaper, with stories and photos created by my students, is the most exciting project I've done in the classroom.

When first graders take pictures and have time to talk about them, write about them, and use them in authentic ways, they learn to trust themselves and their learning in a whole new way. They are impressed with themselves and what they can do. And other people are impressed with them too!

Cameras as a Motivational Tool

Motivation is a key to all learning success in the classroom. Cameras and photographs are paramount motivational tools. Kids are good at learning to use technological resources, and they love to be in charge. When we make cameras available, we provide this opportunity. Children get to look at and record something about their world through their own eyes. And after they take their pictures, they have their own snapshots to validate and acknowledge their personal vision.

Last Thanksgiving, my children showed their expertise as they traveled quietly around the school with me and searched out photos to report on the variety of ways Martin School students were celebrating the holidays. Eileen Christopherson, one of our kindergarten teachers, said she couldn't believe her eyes when my kids came with me to photograph the three-class feast in the cafeteria. As kindergarten children, decked in paper Thanksgiving garb, enjoyed a small meal of cornbread, fruit, popcorn, and other treats, my students walked in proudly to find out what was going on and write about it. One of my girls carried our digital camera, and another child took care of the camera case. After a few minutes, they switched off.

Eileen said, "When your kids are on a reporting mission, they really step up to the plate! Those two little girls were so proud and confident as they carried the equipment, and they took all those photos without help. By the swing in their step, you could tell they were in charge! And the rest of the kids were taking it all in so they could write about it."

The photos my children take and the stories they write give credence and importance to students, events, and activities. I like to think they contribute to school spirit. As one of my first graders, Sagar, says, "If you're a kid, it's really cool when you get in the newspaper, and everybody reads about you and sees your picture. You're kinda famous." Another of my students, Aryanna, concurs: "It's a big deal when you get in the paper."

My principal, Mario Penman, said to me after reading a newspaper edition featuring some upper-grade students, "You have no idea what this photo and story will do for these kids. They've been right on the edge and frequently in trouble; I've felt that they could go either way. Being featured in a schoolwide newspaper in a positive light will help them tremendously!"

Photo Collage—a Simple Project with Great Impact

For many years, before I let students use the cameras in my classroom, I used photography very simply with children: I asked each student to do a special pose for one personal photograph. I had the photo processed (in later years, I printed it myself). Then I cut the photo out and gave it to the student to embellish and write about. I still find these photo collages—with the child's photo incorporated in his drawing—to be amazing creations. The activity is an exciting way to stimulate language, creativity, imagination, self-esteem, and self-fulfillment.

To begin this lesson, I asked children to rev up their imaginations and think about some of their wildest dreams: What would they wish they could do or what would they love to see themselves doing if they could do anything in the world, real or imaginary? As kids individually acted out their hearts' desires, I took their pictures. If a child was going to be flying, swimming, or engaging in a full-length activity, I snapped the photo with the student stretched out on the ground or reaching up. If a child's pose involved sitting—flying an airplane, piloting a rocket ship, taking off in a magic coach or on a magic carpet, driving a car, riding an elephant or a dragon—I took the photo with the child posed on a chair. When the pictures were processed, I cut around children's images and removed any unneeded details, such as the floor or a chair.

My students were so excited to get their photo cutouts. When I handed them out, I stuck a tape roll behind each one and gave children white drawing paper. Kids stuck their pictures anywhere they liked on the page and drew and pasted on the rest of the collage. At a later date I realized it was a good idea to first make several photocopies of these cutout photographic images of students (all of them taped on a single sheet of paper or two), so they could be used again in other ways. Kids enjoy having pictures and photocopies of themselves and their classmates to use in other writing and art projects.

Making Wishes Seem Real

Kelly had freckles, tangled strawberry blond hair, and a dreamy smile. She hadn't been having an easy time in first grade or at home, but at this moment things were going *her* way: Kelly had just drawn a crayon picture of a magic vehicle—a pumpkin coach pulled by white horses. She added a rough figure outside this magic vehicle. The man had his hand extended to his passenger. Kelly completed the illustration by attaching her cutout photograph, centered right in front of the pumpkin's round open doorway. The rudimentary footman she drew was helping her climb aboard. Then she continued working on her story about her best wish: a trip to a fairytale castle.

As Kelly worked, my other first graders created their own fantastic stories featuring *their* cutout photos of themselves. Soriel flew over a burning city, crayoned cape stretched out behind him. Tomás rode a motorcycle drawn with incredible marking pen and crayon details. And Michael hung from the edge of a skyscraper.

Jason put his cutout photo of himself in an ocean he created with colored pens. He added a spouting whale and a sign floating high up on a big wave: "Leave these whales alone!" While Chris captained a pirate ship and Patricia flew in Santa's sleigh to help deliver presents, Marcus pasted his photo on paper and drew a marking pen wetsuit on his image. Then he added a swordfish and many other kinds of sea creatures hovering over the ocean floor. It didn't bother Marcus that he had colored over most of his photographed face with pen to fashion the diving helmet. He reminded me that *he* knew he was inside that black helmet shape!

The images and stories these children created were quite imaginative—the stuff of wishes and dreams. The pictures they made were real to them: when you can see yourself doing something in a photograph, it is easy to believe the impossible can happen.

Although I taught this photo-art-writing project to children in one of my very first classes, I have used these ideas ever since. I remember these kids' images well because this was the first time I had envisioned, planned, and implemented the project, and I was so excited with the results that I made copious notes.

Do the Projects Yourself—*Model, Model, Model*

I worked right along with the children on this newly envisioned project, although I didn't show them my collage until they were all finished. I was as pleased as they were with the results of all our work. And I especially enjoyed my own flying trapeze photo and drawing, since this was something that fascinated me but that I would *never*, ever do.

Children in my classroom in more recent years have come up with slightly different fantastic images, but their illustrations are equally powerful—and lasting! Last June I was touched and surprised when I attended an end-of-the-school-year party at the home of Rosalinda Flores, our office clerk. During the event, I had time to visit with her son, Tomás, my former first-grade student. He showed me two special personal treasures. The first was the aforementioned collage: a combined photograph and drawing (now beautifully framed) that showed six-year old Tomás riding a motorcycle—the project he had created in my class. (See Figure 1–1.)

The second surprise was seeing grown-up Tomás' actual motorcycle and fully equipped automotive workshop in the garage attached to the house.

"I always did want a motorcycle," he reminded me. Tomás is now thirty-six years old. It is touching to me that he still cherishes his special photograph and motorcycle drawing. Tomás truly lives the life he had imagined. My fervent hope is that many of the other students I have taught over the years have had some of *their* visualized dreams come true.

Everything Is Possible

Brainstorming stories and possibilities with children is a powerful motivational strategy. The kids think of ideas way beyond my thoughts, and sharing these ideas

Figure 1–1. Tomás rides the motorcycle he wishes for.

gets their minds working. As Linus Pauling, American theoretical chemist and biologist, and author of *The Nature of the Chemical Bond*, says, "The best way to have a good idea is to have lots of ideas." A traditional rabbinical saying notes, "Don't limit your child to your own learning, for he was born in another time." I want my students to have the chance to think and create without worrying about making mistakes. Edward de Bono, author of over sixty-two books on constructive and creative thinking, including *Lateral Thinking: Creativity Step-by-Step*, expresses this thought well: "It is better to have enough ideas by having some of them be wrong than to be always right by having no ideas at all." After we brainstorm possibilities, kids can't wait to get started on their own individual projects.

Children work on many skills as they take photos and write, organize, talk, and think to create their own personal stories and books. They are honing their writing and storytelling, their organization and thinking skills, and they're developing their own unique and creative imaginations. My students are learning to focus and build on things that matter to them and follow through with creating something uniquely their own. They are motivated by the chance to share these special stories with classmates. As they listen to each other, they give their friends good feedback and encouragement. Our classroom community becomes a school family.

Photos Invite Stories, and Stories Generate Language Practice

Photos call out for stories to be told. As John Fergus-Jean, photographer and educator, says in *Teaching Photography: Tools for the Imaging Educator* (Rand and Zakia 2006, 299), "We bring our stories to images." Children love one-to-one time to talk about their snapshots and share their personal stories with their teacher. It is important to provide group and individual sharing time as well. With photographs as the focus of their stories, kids get authentic, meaningful, and nonthreatening oral language practice in small groups or in a whole-class setting. Photos and tales create rapport between teacher and student, as well as between students and their classmates. And this is one way to find out things about each other we really don't know and wouldn't be likely to learn any other way.

Dick Sperisen, San Mateo County art education coordinator emeritus, links stories with art and other curricula in workshops and presentations he gives. "Stories come alive in the telling," he says. "We use the camera eye to see and to have something to talk about. Until they have had some drawing experiences and opportunities to put pencil to paper, some kids might say, 'I can't draw.' The camera gives them another way to have success." (I have known Dick for many years and have attended several of his workshops and presentations. I doubt very much that there has ever been anyone in his workshops who wasn't inspired to draw.) But, as Dick says, photos and photo collage are additional incentives for drawing, self-expression, and other skills. "Art and storytelling are the road to reading," he says.

Teacher Notes and Snaps

I like to take photographs of children that go with some of the special things they say. And I keep a notebook for writing these gems down immediately so I get their words verbatim. I noticed that one of my children always projected an aura of serenity and well-being. One day, as we walked to class, he raised his head and took a deep breath. "Ah, sweet air," he said. "Sometimes it smells like water." I scribbled his words down on scrap paper as we walked, and later that day as we were heading for the cafeteria, I took his picture to go with his words. He put both items in his photo album–memory book. I would never have believed children could come

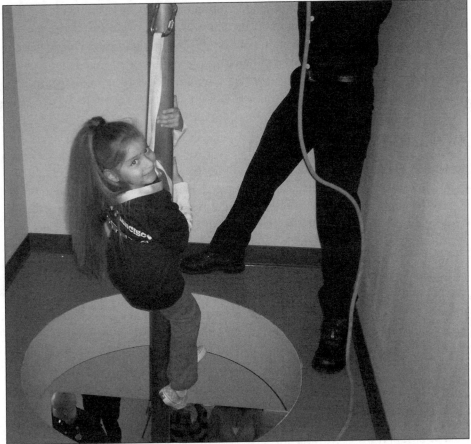

Figure 1–2. Aryanna slides down the fire pole.

up with some of their wonderfully expressed thoughts if I hadn't been jotting them down immediately.

The sense of wonder and gladness children feel and convey is one of their best, truest gifts. Part of my job is to honor their feelings and thoughts and help preserve these for them. Photographs conserve those special moments for the children as well.

When one of my children, Aryanna, won a districtwide grand prize in a fire department–sponsored poster contest, she was invited to lunch at the local firehouse. Since timing made it impossible for me to attend, I gave her one of the digital cameras to take with her to record the event. Her photos convey a lot of information about the award celebration and luncheon and many details about firehouse life: checking out the neighborhood on a fire truck, training a resident firedog, and cooking for the firehouse crew. My favorite photo, and one Aryanna chose to write about, shows her strapping into a big yellow belt and fearlessly sliding down the fire pole! She had told me she was going to do this if she got the chance, and she was deservedly proud of herself. The firefighters had made her day by telling her what a good job she did and how brave she was! (See Figure 1–2.)

The class was fascinated by Aryanna's tale of her visit to the fire department. The children chose to make this the lead story in our next school newspaper.

An Idea Can Take Off!

As with Aryanna, when one child gets a brainstorm or has a momentous achievement, it can involve us all. Marlo fantasized in detail about a photograph he wished he could take for a story he wanted to write and tell. As his story evolved, he brought us along with him for the ride: "All of us in room 7 are on a spaceship. We're going inside the moon," he said. Marlo wanted his photo to show "what it looks like in there." He used pens and crayons to work out the details of what it really would look like in his "moon room," and then he finished the image by affixing cutout photos of friends, classmates, and the teacher to his large inside-the-moon drawing. The children and I were intrigued. They added more adventures to the story, with Marlo's permission. This turned into an exciting tale and a class big book! Every time we read the story we inhabited it. The story voice and the story became *ours*, and we lived the adventure together.

Before the year was out, Marlo became a main prizewinner in a countywide SamTrans bus contest. His artwork is now displayed on the outside of a bus, and his photograph is on the bus as well; it shows him holding his art. Marlo was honored at a SamTrans event and was given a certificate of achievement at a South San Francisco City Council meeting. City Councilwoman Karyl Matsumoto arranged the award from the city and praised Marlo's achievement. Marlo's comment to me was that he hoped this story and photo would be in our room 7 newspaper. Naturally, it was our next lead story!

The Photo-Art-Language Connection for English Language Learners
Edward's Breakthrough

Edward is an English learner who uses his great command of crayons and pens to express himself. For example, Edward draws an intricate picture of his friend Hector, a photograph he wants someone to take: "Me and Hector are doing something in the world. Good. Special," he tells us.

Edward uses a cutout photo of himself and another one of Hector when he works to illustrate his story. He fastens the photos to art paper with tape rolls on the back and then draws the rest of the picture. Now he's ready to tell his story to the group.

As Edward's language evolves, he will be able to tell us more about his unique contribution to the world. For now, while I wonder, I note that he really feels proud of himself as he spins his tale. He is using more language describing his special adventure than he has at any time since school started, as he tells this incomplete but highly successful personal story.

Hector's Photo Story

When Hector shared a photograph of his father, he talked about his dad and how much he likes being with him. He told us about his father's unusual hobby: making circus balloons. "I like to sit with my Dad," Hector told us. "He can blow balloons and make lotsa stuff with them." As Hector talked, he conveyed the excitement he feels when he anticipates the different animals his father will create by simple twists and turns and combinations of balloons.

The children were so intrigued by Hector's story that they decided to invite Hector's father to class for an interview and to watch him demonstrate his talent with balloons. We all had a great time watching Mauricio León make long, thin balloons metamorphose into animals and flowers. It was apparent to all of us that Hector had gotten just as good at this craft as his dad and that they loved to work together. The whole class ultimately learned to create balloon figures. The kids interviewed Hector's father and wrote about the experience both in our school newspaper and in a web book titled *Our Balloon Man*. (For more on web books and a sample page of this book, see Chapter 5.)

It was especially moving to me to find out that Hector's dad had *not* previously known how to create these balloons. He had taught himself how to do this craft in order to back up his son's story and because he didn't want to disappoint him. Mr. León's wonderful presentation gave Hector a great deal of prestige and recognition in the classroom. The whole project gave Hector self-confidence too. When I asked him how he learned to make the balloons, he said, "The more you do it, the more you get better."

Rudy's Struggle

Rudy was a late-year addition to our classroom. He spoke no English, and because he had some language difficulties, he spoke very little Spanish. Most of the time he communicated with us through his art or through single words that were somewhat difficult to understand. Speech classes began to help him. Photography was another resource for him. He was so excited about sharing his photos and the stories that went with them that he took huge risks to try to express himself.

Rudy wrote a story I could not figure out at first. Nor could I quite understand his reading of it. His words were not very clearly spoken in either language. He had the choice of writing Spanish, but he had elected to write in English. I finally asked

Rudy to come to the computer with me, and as he read his story, I typed what I thought I heard. He grew more and more confident as he spoke, and as his voice grew stronger and I became familiar with his language rhythm, I began to understand what I was hearing. The way he read his work made it sound like a story poem. I read my typing back to Rudy, and he corrected my mistakes. Going back and forth like this, we ended up with the following text, which he read in a loud voice with great intensity. He illustrated his work with his own dinosaur photo and artwork to make a story collage. It all felt like a major breakthrough.

Rudy's original written text (without any corrections or changes) read:

> Famel Go The dog Go Go Go
> t-red Go The Famel dog GoGo
> famel GoGo GoGoGo the t-red
> Name blue.

When Rudy came to the computer, he dictated the following to me, in an impassioned voice. He was really into his story. (Note: I have made no changes in his story. I put punctuation where his voice indicated it should go.)

> My family running. The dog running running running.
> T-rex running. He running. My family running.
> Name Blue.

Meaning was clearer to me now, and the hair on the back of my neck stood up. This child's voice was so urgent that the story seemed real. I wondered whether Rudy and his family had experienced some real danger.

Rudy dictated the final version of his story in Spanish. (Once again, I made no changes in his story and guessed as to where to put punctuation.)

> Mi familia está corriendo, corriendo, corriendo.
> El perro está corriendo.
> T-rex está corriendo adelante de mi familia.
> Su nombre es Azul.

I got a slight bit more information in this version of Rudy's story. I learned that the T-rex is running after Rudy's family and the dog (which was implied in his written version and the English dictation). And I learned from the last sentence, which translates to "His name is Blue," that this is the name of the dinosaur, something that was hinted at in earlier versions of the tale.

I was exhausted by this effort to understand, made more challenging by this student's speech production difficulties, and Rudy was equally tired from the gigantic effort of trying to make himself understood. But he was determined to complete his story and use it with a photo he had taken at the Lawrence Hall of Science dinosaur exhibit. Rudy did not give up, and he was patient with my efforts to type his story the way he wanted it. It was important to both of us that his work was printed out as he had envisioned it, and we were both elated when we finished the job.

I have found that when children speak from their own hearts, with intensity and fervor, with images to back up their words, they can generally make themselves understood. Difficulties with grammar, syntax, and even production of speech sounds just don't get in their way!

Photos can capture children's interests and passions and show these in ways even words cannot. These pictures help validate for kids what they see as important and help them become active, involved learners in our classroom. As photographer and educator Sean Perry notes in *Teaching Photography: Tools for the Imaging Educator* (Rand and Zakia 2006, 303), "Photography is about getting to the heart of an image." This photography project takes me to the heart of children's lives, hopes, and dreams and enables me to use the things I learn to teach more effectively. Children construct meaning when they see their photographs. Their work is intensely personal and authentic. These experiences with writing, art, and photography help ignite their learning and clarify their individual ambitions and aspirations, in and out of school.

2

Simple Camera Projects
for Home and School

I don't think I'd remember anything at all . . . if I didn't have pictures.
—Abigail Breslin, fifth-grade star of *Little Miss Sunshine,*
as quoted in a television ad

"I'm going to take pictures of my daddy and mommy holding hands," Betsy said when she learned that she could bring a disposable camera home to take photos. Frederick's mother had just undergone serious surgery. "I want to take pictures of my dad helping my mom walk again," Frederick said. And another child decided his photos of choice would be of himself so his parents, whom he never sees, could "know what [he] look[s] like."

When my first graders sat with me in front of an easel tablet and listed photos they wished they could take, their ideas took my breath away. I shared some of my choices with them too, including some pictures I wished someone had taken when I was small: my little brother Jimmy posing as the Polite Cowboy in his black hat, black denim jacket, jeans, and boots (in 100-plus-degree heat) and a picture of me riding my bike with my braids swinging out and Dutchie, our border collie, loping along beside me. I also wish I had a photo of my eight-year-old sister Sherry blithely cooking the Christmas Eve steak we had purchased with our allowances—she cooked the treat for our dog—while the family ate casserole for dinner. I still remember my dad saying, "There's something wrong with this picture." My mom just smiled and shook her head. But these are only pictures in my mind, not actual photographs in an album or a frame.

My Life in Snaps

Before my students take disposable cameras home to take *their* pictures, I share with them two or three personal photographs, a couple of them from my early-school and pre-school days. I am trying to make the point with the children that a seemingly ordinary photograph can capture a special slice of life. Something that

16

doesn't seem remarkable or particular in any way might be an image we would like to preserve forever. The kids love to talk about my pictures and guess as much as they can from each photo. We can all view these better for class discussion when I reproduce them as acetates to share on the overhead projector.

As children look at the first photo, they decide that I am the elder of the two small children playing a game on the rug, that the other child must be my sister, and that she is mad. They figure out that it must be because I am winning the game. The children call my sister Sherry *la enojada*, which translates to "the angry one" in Spanish. This is news to me. I actually don't view the photo that way. What I like about the picture is that it shows us playing much the way we always did. It's just one picture representing hundreds of other moments.

My first graders especially love the photo of me, at two, holding onto a children's book. They know me well enough to think this is a good and apt representation and that perhaps I haven't changed much. Now they puzzle over one of my other photographs. They cannot figure out why I find this photo of the white-haired woman talking on the telephone to be really unusual. They guess, correctly, that this is my mother. I explain that she was totally deaf until she had an operation at age seventy-nine to restore some hearing. This picture shows the first time she could ever hear well enough to talk with my brother on the telephone. Now the children, too, see that this is an image of a truly extraordinary event, one to be celebrated and treasured.

The kids love making their own lists of photos to take. They keep these in their binders and update them on a regular basis, adding new ideas as they occur to them. Luis' list, shown in Figure 2–1, shows his thinking quite clearly. He has incorporated drawings with his writing as he figures out his plan to capture fish and turtles on camera—and maybe a lion.

Linking Home and School with Photographs and Writing: Personal Memoir

My goal for my students when I purchase disposable cameras is to give them opportunities to take photos and use them to tell *their* special life stories. I want to give children the chance to create something they will value—something particularly their own. I give each child a memory album binder with several plastic page protectors for holding writing and photos. We take our time with this project and work on it all year. I provide different templates with photo boxes and lines and blank paper of assorted colors. Children work at their own pace in their own ways to mount photos (with tape rolls on the back or glue sticks), write about their pictures, and tell about the things they have seen and experienced. The results are poignant and very personal. The writing is inspired because children are telling intense stories that matter to them.

Figure 2–1. Luis hoped to take pictures of several animals.

A *few* photos go a long way. The first year I provided disposable cameras to my first-grade class (aided by a wonderful and generous donor!), each child had a camera and took all twenty-seven photos. I found that this amount of photos was both more expensive to process and more cumbersome to work with than necessary. Since that time, we have used class digital cameras in school and on the playground and *shared* the disposable cameras that went home. Each child takes six or seven pictures on these single-use cameras. This is a good balance of photographs. Children get a variety of photographic experiences and can follow their interests as to what photographs they choose to take (or pose for).

If my students had access to digital cameras at home, I would encourage them to use the cameras for this project, but no one in my classes yet has had a personal camera available. One or two photographs per child—or even photocopies from our school picture—are enough to get this project started.

When I was experimenting with a sample album, for my eyes only, photos were mounted straight, the colored background paper was coordinated, the papers were encased in plastic page protectors, and I thought it all looked pretty good. But I have to say with emphasis, *the children's work looks even better*. It reflects their growing small-motor achievements, their developing personal tastes, their ages, and their personalities. These pages, like the photos on them, could only be made by them—priceless artifacts to look at in future years.

Telling stories with photographs can be more evocative and moving than just using words. When children take photos important to them, they can't wait to tell their stories. They dive right into the writing, and the results are true, poignant, and full of special childhood memories and meaning. One of Edward's first creative endeavors is a photo and story about his brand-new four-pound baby sister, Karyl. He writes the story at home with a little help from mom but does many similar pieces of writing at school.

Several children have pictures taken of themselves reading to someone in their family at home. Other common themes are brothers and sisters, friends, and pets. Alfonso takes pictures of everyone in his family reading to everyone else. We use these on a chart with an adaptation of the words of poet Strickland Gillian ("The Reading Mother," *Best Loved Poems of the American People*, Felleman and Allen 1936): "Richer than I you could never be. I have a *family* that reads to me!" We add on photos of other children being read to by family members.

Daniel works hard for several days during writers workshop and writes a poignant piece about his father:

> My Dad's name is Ruben. My dad is kind. I love him. I kiss my dad. He is funny. He makes jokes. He is hardworking. My dad is nice. He is the best. My dad has light skin and black eyes. He works at Sky Chef.

At a later date, Daniel draws a picture of his dad and then takes his photograph.

Luis and some other children decide they need a photo of King Betta, our new Indonesian fighting fish, and they arrange a little group and choose a class photographer to take their picture together. Since the camera and printing dock are new, we all find it truly amazing that we are able to place the digital camera on the printing dock and watch a mini printing press create the photo—first the yellow ink, then magenta, cyan, and black. The fish is clearly visible, and we are all agog and energized. Ultimately, Luis writes about the photo and creates a collage page about it, incorporating the classroom aquarium setup and his own experiences with fish, as seen in Figure 2–2.

Thrilled with our new camera, the first digital camera we have used, kids group together and figure out snaps to take of each other: Rodolfo with the American flag he made from scraps and found objects, Frederick in his brand-new glasses, and Alberto, barely visible behind his SpongeBob SquarePants shades. The boys love figuring out their group arrangement and posing for the class photographer they have chosen.

It seems a small thing, but I know the behind-the-scenes stories on all of it. Luis knows a great deal about aquariums and fish, and he is happy to share his expertise. I see how Rodolfo guards and lines up his art supplies, saves bits and pieces of everyone's trash, and bursts with excitement and inspiration to put them together to create something new. I've been aware all morning of Frederick's pride in his new glasses. Who could miss it? He's polished them twelve times and remarked about how well he can see now. And Alberto has been gloating over his "shades" for days. The boys have come together to showcase their friendship and parts of their lives that matter. And now these vignettes are memorialized visually, and they each have a copy of the image.

Frederick can reminisce, years later, and perhaps remember that this was the day he got his eyeglasses. Rodolfo may look back and feel that frisson when he put junk together to create something he was proud of, something everyone else wished they could make too. And Alberto may recall getting to be in a photo with two boys he liked as friends and finally getting to wear his square-lens SpongeBob sunglasses in the classroom. Luis might even remember that he helped set up our class aquarium and created a photo collage. With luck, he might still have it.

Children's Choices

Photos the children take can be serious or playful, and choices are left entirely up to them except for one request: I ask, when I introduce this project at parent conferences in October, that one photo be taken of someone at home reading to each

Figure 2–2. Luis' photo collage.

child. I feel strongly about the importance of this parent-child read-aloud time and want to emphasize it to children's parents when we meet together. I feel that just having this photo and looking at it will help us celebrate this all-important daily ritual.

I make copies of these read-aloud photos and we create another class display: "It's Magic When Someone Reads to Us." The chart is a wonderful visual to have up in our classroom. There is something so satisfying about seeing each child being read to at home.

Ways to Learn About Children

I believe that the more we observe children, pay attention to their interests and to the things they say and do, the greater our ability to teach them well. We can hone our lessons to suit their ways of thinking and learning. And children, especially English learners who have some communication difficulties as they gain facility in the language, use cameras as a way to value and share their lives. Through this photography and writing project, I learn a lot about children's families. These connections help children see that I really am interested in their personal lives, and I care about them. They bloom as they share with me and with the class.

Of course, I always try to remain sensitive to the child who may not wish to open up in this way. The choice is totally the child's.

How to Lead Up to the Project

Before I introduce the photography memory book project to my students, I give them some very elementary background in photography and in memoir. We talk about how everyday events can really be special moments. I read books like *Family Pictures/Cuadros de familia*, by Carmen Lomas Garza (1990). Children love the big book edition of this picture book. Each double-page spread has a large painting by the author-illustrator on one side and a paragraph about her life as a child on the other side. My students love to look at the paintings for clues and find out all they can about the author when she was small. Then, when we read the matching paragraph together, they can check on their understandings and congratulate themselves on their clever detective work in ferreting out meaning from a painting. Some other special books we enjoy are *In My Family/En mí familia* (Garza 2000) and *Magic Windows/Ventanas mágicas* (Garza 2003). Other favorite memoirs are *My Diary from Here to There/Mi diario de aquí hasta allá*, by Amanda Irma Perez (2002), *Abuela*, by Arthur Dorros (1997), and *I Like Saturdays y Domingos*, by Alma Flor Ada (2004). Children also like picture books illustrated with photographs, such as *Immigrant Kids* (2006), *Children of the Wild West* (1990), and *Kids at Work: Lewis Hine and the Crusade Against Child Labor* (1998), all by Russell Freedman.

Exposure to Great Photographers

Recently our interest in photography took a scholarly turn. My dear friend Marsha Oviatt took a National Geographic trip to Antarctica and met the renowned photographer Paul Nicklen aboard ship. Since I had the ship's itinerary, my children tracked my friend's progress on the large world map and read about Antarctica with me during her journey. When Marsha returned, she brought a special *National Geographic* magazine for our class. It featured Nicklen's photos of penguins and leopard seals in Antarctica in an article by Kim Heacox: "Deadly Beauty: A Photographer Falls Under the Spell of Antarctica's Leopard Seals" (2006). Best of all, there was a personal letter to us from Paul Nicklen, written on the pertinent magazine pages. The letter commended the children on their interest in Antarctica and expressed Nicklen's wish that they too would someday visit "the most beautiful place on earth."

Making a Collage for the Overhead Projector

One of the ways my kids visited Antarctica vicariously was by making a movable collage on the overhead projector. I photocopied and enlarged some photos from a commercial travel pamphlet on Antarctica and turned them into overhead transparencies. I also made (and cut out) overhead transparencies from photographs of my students. In this way, children could create their own visual experiences aboard ship, on an iceberg, standing next to a penguin, and so on, by placing one cut transparency on top of another. When Jacelynn placed a transparency of a photo of herself next to one of an adelie penguin, it looked as if they were standing together on a glacier. We could take our acetate images off the National Geographic ship, *Endeavor*, and put ourselves aboard a rubber boat called a Zodiak en route to land. We made many creative photo stories in this way.

This was a great large-group project and an even better small-group learning center. Four children at a time got to move the overhead transparencies around and create and tell their own stories. These experiences gave great oral language practice, provided good language support to English learners, and led to some strong writing as well!

A Visit from an Antarctic Traveler

My class was quite fortunate to have a visit from my friend Marsha upon her return from Antarctica. The Penguin Lady, as my children call her, showed them slides of her trip, especially of icebergs, bergie bits—tiny pieces of icebergs—and best of all, penguins! Marsha brought us ice cream (to remind us of the temperatures at the South Pole), a book on emperor penguins, and lots of information about four different species of penguins. By the time she left, the kids could easily identify each species and had learned a lot about life on the world's southernmost continent!

Marsha also contributed to the children's projects in another important way. She gave our class a digital camera that she and her husband, Nevin, were no longer using. This gave us even more opportunities to take photos!

The kids achieved a little notoriety from this area of study as well. Our office staff always keeps a current edition of our school newspaper (see Chapter 6) in the office window. The headline in one December issue read, "Our Letter from Antarctica!" It detailed a photocopy of the letter we had received and information about Paul Nicklen and his leopard seal photography project. As we passed by the office at lunchtime, we saw a little group of older students reading our paper. I heard one of them say, "How do they *do* that? How did they get a letter all the way from Antarctica?" I enjoyed the exchange.

A Website Visit

After absorbing the *National Geographic* article and Nicklen's photos of leopard seals, my first graders and I visited his website and perused his wondrous gallery of photographs. Since the timing was just before Christmas, my students particularly enjoyed photos of the Arctic and the northern lights, up near the North Pole. I overheard the kids talking animatedly about Paul Nicklen's photographs, especially those of the leopard seals, the penguins, and the "rainbows" in the sky, the northern lights. Exposure to the work of this great photographer had truly fueled their imaginations.

Children have other opportunities to study photographs and learn about famous photographers and photography as a career. One of the camera-related learning centers I organize (see Chapter 8) provides a variety of photographic books and magazines to study and talk about together. See the "References and Resources" section at the end of this book for lists of photography books and books with photographic illustrations.

A book we all particularly enjoyed is *Come Look with Me: Discovering Photographs with Children*, by Jean S. Tucker (1994), an art and photographic historian. The book showcases the work of twelve famous photographers. Each photo is accompanied by open-ended questions and text explaining the photographer's ideas and the story of how each picture came to be taken. "Chuckie," a photo taken by Joel Meyerowitz on Cape Cod, shows a young boy carrying a large bluefish on his shoulders. At first glance, the fish appears to be growing out of the boy's neck. Another favorite photo in my classes is "Drum Major and Children," taken by *Life* magazine photographer Alfred Eisenstaedt. The image creates a great picture story. Children love the fact that a group of seven kids are following a strutting drum major across a field, mimicking everything he does, while he doesn't appear to know this is going on.

I introduced the children to some photos in *Philippe Halsman's Jump Book* (1986). Halsman, who did 101 *Life* magazine covers, discovered a unique way to relax his subjects: he asked them to jump! The children and I have tried this technique with mixed results. It is difficult to get everybody's head in the picture while shooting even a small group of children jumping when using an inexpensive digital camera. But once in a while, we get some fun photos, and certainly everyone is *relaxed* when we try this technique!

Perhaps the children's favorite photographer is John Drysdale, whose work is collected in *Our Peaceable Kingdom: The Photographs of John Drysdale*, a book compiled and introduced by Margaret Regan (2000). Drysdale photographs children and animals, often together, and some of the pictures are hilarious: a child walking a crocodile, a little girl whispering a secret to an elephant, and even a boy and a horse reading together. See also *Tricky Pix*, by Paula Weed and Carla Jimison (2001), and *The Kid's Arts and Crafts Book*, by Patricia Petrich (my former name) and Rosemary Dalton (1975), for some ideas for tricks with photographs. I use photos from these books to encourage children to talk and tell stories (see Chapter 8, "Imagination Stations").

I also have introduced my first graders, as well as the intermediate after-school class I teach, to the still-life photography of Ansel Adams, using the children's biography *Ansel Adams: America's Photographer*, by Beverly Gherman (2002). This has fueled their interest in photographing landscapes.

My Real Focal Point

Whether we are learning about photographers or taking our own photos, the heart of this photography project for me is my focus on understanding children and paying attention to what they do, what they say, and how they follow their passions and interests and how they learn. The skills and understandings that come about from working with cameras and photos this way transfer to other areas of the curriculum. Getting a chance to work on personal projects of their own choosing makes children feel their ideas and interests have value and spurs them on to enjoy learning and to grow.

Kayla's List

When Kayla takes her disposable camera home, she has a big agenda! The next day, she bounces back into the classroom full of the camera experience. She lists in detail exactly what photos were taken, all of them of her except for one that includes her mother, pregnant with Kayla's little sister. Kayla's camera litany is so fascinating that I grab a pen and write down the list of her photos on large easel paper. Kayla doesn't stop talking until all photos are listed and the giant tablet page is full!

When we read the list together, I realize that Kayla has led her family on a merry chase with that camera! Photos showcase her doing gymnastics, making cookies, jumping rope, playing with dolls with her friend, listening for her unborn sister, with her ear to her pregnant mom's stomach, and saying her prayers.

This was a lot of information to commit to memory, but Kayla had it all down pat. It was good that she did. Within two weeks, as we waited for the rest of the shared cameras to be returned so the film could be developed, our classroom was broken into, and all the cameras were stolen. It was a heartbreaking moment in my first-grade classroom.

In a journal excerpt on that date, I wrote:

Today was a sad day. When the children and I came back to school after a school holiday, we found that our classroom had been broken into. All our disposable cameras were missing—most of them chock-full of precious memories and special events. These missing cameras included the seven or eight disposable class cameras we'd used together since September (with Parent Conference photos of each child and parent, some Back to School Night photos) and all the cameras the kids had taken home—full of their own special pictures. The after school enrichment program cameras were missing as well.

I had gathered all the cameras in a bunch at my chair in order to take them in to have the film developed. Two children hadn't returned cameras, so I decided to wait and only make one camera store trip. But today, the whole pile of cameras was missing—a result of a 2:30 a.m. break-in during a day off school.

Children Vent Their Disappointment

"Oh, no! Our pictures!" the kids moaned. "But I took a picture of my mom and dad holding hands," Betsy said. This sparked a whole-group remembrance of favorite pictures taken and lost: Kayla saying her prayers, Mario's birthday piñata; Frederick's dad helping his mom walk again after her surgery; Mickey playing baseball with his dad; and many other special images. Nothing remained of these captured moments. Or so I thought.

My first graders were tremendously upset, and I was devastated by this loss as well. I tried to make myself feel better by silently reasoning that even though we lost our cameras, my students still *experienced* the process of deciding which photos to take, composing images, executing the photo shoots—and that they had the images of the photos they had taken in their minds' eyes. I really felt the only thing

I could do was to purchase more cameras. Before I could linger on my musings, though, one child had already decided that something had to be done!

My Kids Don't Give Up

At an impromptu class meeting, Sammy led the discussion about what we should do. "We gotta stand up for ourselves," he said.

"Yeah!" several kids said. "We won't give up," they said. This became our new class slogan.

"We could write the sad thing story," Betsy said. So that's what we did. I took dictation, the kids helped me spell, and the children poured all their feelings about the loss onto large sheets of tablet paper. I agreed that we could get more cameras. Kayla and a few other children thought of even more photos they could take. Kayla had an especially good reason for another photo shoot: Now she could take some pictures of the new baby when it came!

Kids wrote and talked and vented their unhappiness. We reread our "Sad Thing Story" together.

The Sad Thing Story

On vacation some kids got in our special class and they stole our cameras. We took special pictures and we like our special pictures. We feel angry, sad, upset.

They stole our pictures.

But we're not gonna give up! We will take the pictures again!

At another time, we would revise, expand, and illustrate our story. Today it seemed to serve a great purpose: it used up a lot of our sad energy and gave us a way to cope.

Later in the day, I read the children an Aesop fable. As I customarily do when I share read-aloud text with no pictures, I made a storyboard on the whiteboard: six outlined boxes with a few lines for text underneath each one. I drew pictures in sequence as I read and told the tale. A great idea seemed to dawn on all of us at about the same moment: "Let's make storyboards! Let's draw our pictures so we remember them!" the kids shouted.

This brainstorm seemed to buoy us up, give us yet another mechanism for dealing with our loss. Children began drawing their "Lost Pictures" storyboards and thinking about what was special about their photos. They were moving ahead, working to leave loss behind.

The next day the kids added this line to their group tale, "The Sad Thing Story": "We'll make storyboards and remember our pictures."

It took several days for children to complete their storyboards. The storyboard template I usually give them has six boxes measuring about 4 inches by 5 inches, with four lines under each box. The boxes fit on large 14-by-17-inch ledger-sized

Figure 2–3. Lupita's storyboad about being a photographer.

paper horizontally, in two rows, three boxes to a row. Lupita had completed only two blocks out of six. Rather than write about her lost pictures, she began with a positive topic: "How to Be a Photographer." Since Lupita entered first grade speaking very little English, her speaking and writing, while very evocative, would be hard to understand and decipher. See Figure 2–3 for the beginning of her storyboard and my transcription of her story.

Lupita had written:

How to Be a Photographer

When a photographer takes your picture you just look like the photographer was not there.

Lupita was referring to my request of my students when I take their pictures. I ask them to just go on with what they are doing and pretend I am invisible.

The Sequel to Our "Sad Thing Story"

When our principal offered to replace the cameras that I had purchased, the children were fired up again to move ahead. They came up with ideas for additional photos, as well as those they wanted to retake. By the following week, students were taking pictures again and making new plans. Maybe even more than their precious photos, what the kids learned from this experience is the importance of perseverance. Even in the midst of great disappointment, they didn't give up.

I'm now quite sure that my children's spirit of going forward with the project was a more important lesson than even the photos would have been. It helped me

Figure 2–4. Eliana's piece on perseverance.

get over my own disappointment to hear them say, "We should stand up for ourselves! We should keep doing it. We should take pictures again. We won't give up!"

Eliana put this philosophy of assertiveness into print and a drawing. (I confess to having worked hard on teaching this philosophy all year long, and I had shared some personal stories.) Figure 2–4 shows her work.

Comparing the Work

After children had taken a second round of pictures to replace those in the stolen cameras, I asked each one privately, "Did you get the pictures you wanted? Do you like these as well as the other pictures in the missing cameras?" Except for one or two who hesitated in answering, most of the children answered yes, they got the photos they wanted. Most of them didn't seem to mind anymore that some of their pictures were lost.

However, in retrospect, I think perhaps they just gave me the answer I'd be most comfortable with.

I'll never know which were best—the shots taken in the spirit of adventure and the new experience and excitement of using a camera, or the photos taken with retrospection and a little bit of experience. I wish we had both sets of images to compare.

Sammy's Tree

Some children lose book bags and homework under their beds, at the bottom of a toy box, or under a mixed pile of papers, jackets, games, and junk. Kids who have dogs have a myriad of ready-made excuses for lost items, but Sammy's story is my personal favorite. With his grandpa Mike's help when one of our disposable cameras went missing, Sammy found it on the third branch from the top of a tall tree in his backyard. Sammy told me this was his special secret spot.

The fact that Sammy's camera was lost at all was a deeply kept secret I learned of by accident. I was intrigued when I overheard a few comments about the incident. I wanted to know the whole story, so I nudged Sammy into telling it to me at the computer, and I typed as he told me the tale. I wrote it the way he spoke, putting in periods and commas just as his voice indicated. Sammy named the story when he finished, and we reread it together.

Sammy's Tree Story

I took a picture of my papa, Lydia and my brother holding hands all together. I took a picture of my grandma and my dad.

I took a picture in the tree—my house tree. In the tree it was cool climbing it—just me and my big tree.

I was thinking when I was up there. I was telling Mikie my big brother to come so I could take a picture of him like being really small down there.

Always he's bigger, but not when I was in the tree.

And then I left the camera because I forgot it in the tree. Then I lost it! And the next day I climbed my tree and the camera was there.

The day after Sammy told me his tree story, he handed me a crumpled note and a brand-new disposable camera. Yet again, he had lost the camera he left in the tree!

The note said:

I am sorry
I lost it

I bot a nathr wan.
—Sammy

Later that week, with photos from the second camera, Sammy created a photo collage. It showed a cutout snapshot of Sammy holding a camera. It was pasted onto a photo of his tree. The bottom part of this cutout photo resembled a plastic half circle, so Sammy's writing changed to tell the story of his flying-saucer trip to the tree. He modified both his photography and his writing as he worked with his project and created his own uniquely illustrated story.

Sammy was quite pleased with his collage and story, and his cut-and-paste image inspired other children to try photo collage.

3

Kids Behind the Cameras
Going Digital

In order to experience powerful moments in people's lives,
You need to be there when they unfold.
And if you're not, then you just don't see.
—Vicky Allen, photographer

Look What I Can Do!

"Look, teacher! I can play this game from the literacy lab!"
  "I took this hard, hard book home and I can read it!"
  "I made this game with my sister."
  "My mom helped me, and I wrote this story!"
More often than not, multiple stupendous events are happening with your group of children, and they want to tell you about them immediately, the minute they see you approach the class line outside in the morning or the moment you all enter the classroom. This *is* the best time for finding out about these special accomplishments, problems, and thoughts, but it can be a frantic way to start the day since everyone wants to tell you things at once. I do try to listen to everyone's important news as soon as possible, striving for a low-key, informal class climate, as we put things away and get ready to begin our day.

First of all, it's great to be greeted with such excitement and joy. Secondly, if children don't tell you things when they are thrilled to bursting, you may not find out about them. Sometimes news just doesn't have the same import later in the day. It's just not news anymore.

Catch Them at the Celebratory Moment!

The digital camera can play a big part in celebrating moments of achievement, accomplishment, and just plain "need to tell." I try to keep the class digital cameras ready to photograph these moments. The children and I all use the camera in this way. I select photos to be printed right away, put the camera on the printing dock that came with it, and within minutes place these snapshots in a place of

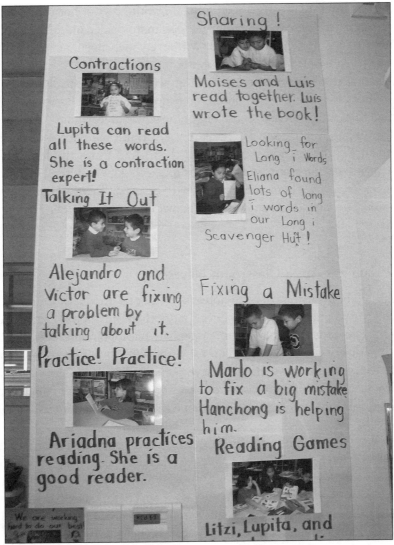

Figure 3–1. "Catch-em being good" photo collection.

honor in our growing photographic display. When we acknowledge special moments with a photograph, we can celebrate again and again.

When we have something significant to celebrate together, I ask my class to meet me at the rug, or sometimes a child will request this. We all look at our brand-new photos, and I mount each one on a piece of light, bright construction paper, such as a 12-inch square. The kids invent the captions, we pop on the photos, and then we read and celebrate together. We take a moment or two to see Litzi play her literary game, listen to Aryanna read a small favorite part of her tricky overnight book, check out the new vowel card game Alejandro made, and listen to part of a story that Ariadna worked on at home. With everyone valued, accepted, and patted on the back, we are ready to go on with our day.

Collecting these special moments of growth photographically makes us all aware of them as we look at the photos and captions on our classroom walls. But more than that, we all become conscious of the power of learning and what it feels like to strive to do our best. The children and I all take photos of the special achievements of others, and we delight in them. And this attitude in the classroom strengthens our group and moves us to excel. The children become aware that others care about them and want them to succeed. We're all pulling for each other—and our digital camera makes this whole learning celebration possible. (See Figure 3–1.)

Digital Cameras Are a Classroom Necessity

Everything about using photography in the classroom is enhanced and improved with digital cameras. You need more than one digital camera because half the excitement of using digital cameras is photographing kids taking pictures. Experiments are the way to go because there is no film to buy, and it is possible to try things out without worrying about the expense of development costs. We just delete the photos we don't want to keep. Digital cameras enable students to get lots of practice as they hone their abilities and develop picture-taking skills.

One way of beginning photography instruction before you even purchase a camera is to teach composition by giving each child a paper camera made from an index card with a one-inch square cut out where the lens would be. (I cut these small squares with a craft knife.) We take these practice cameras on nature walks and brief trips around school and the playground. Students easily compose pictures by looking through the square. They soon get the hang of moving the card closer to and farther from their eyes to change the focus on scenes they could shoot with a camera. Kids soon realize that there are many ways to frame a photograph and that some of them are more effective than others.

Getting Comfortable with a Camera

Before my children take pictures, they need some time to explore with a real camera. I show them the viewfinder, where we frame the pictures we take. They take turns holding cameras, and I talk about the importance of keeping fingers off the camera lens and the LCD. (The lens is like your eye; it needs to see!) We practice

Figure 3–2. Children love taking pictures together.

standing very still as we press the shutter button. Later on, I will have them practice holding the button halfway down, to focus, before they take a picture.

The kids are also briefed about the importance of wearing the wrist strap or neck strap so that we don't drop cameras and damage them. I show them how to turn the camera on and off and how to put it away when it is not in use. I also show them the batteries and talk about the need to conserve them by not leaving an unused camera turned on.

It doesn't take long for children to become adept at picture taking and using the camera. Photography fosters collaborative learning, as Sagar and Níceforo demonstrate as they work together to take a photo. (See Figure 3–2.)

Through Ramiro Orta, Apple computer trainer and professional photographer, I have taken several one-on-one computer, technology, and digital camera classes. Ramiro's wife is a former middle school teacher who instructs students in many subjects, including photography, in Burlingame, California. Ramiro taught his wife's sixth-, seventh-, and eighth-grade students some important tips for taking good pictures. I found these suggestions easy to pass on to my first graders as well as the intermediate-level students in my after-school enrichment class.

Ramiro's Quick Tips

1. Close! Close! Closer! Get as close to your subject as you can before you take the picture. When students get closer to their subject, photos are far more meaningful and interesting.

2. Take pictures of things that matter to you. We all see with our own eyes. The pictures you take will be as unique as you are!

3. Fill the frame and take the picture without hesitation. Ramiro tells students not to hesitate, but to *quickly* take the picture. He feels that lack of inhibition is the main reason that children's photos are frequently better than those of adults. "Kids aren't afraid to just to go up to somebody and take a picture," he says. "They don't care whether they invade your space! When we take the photo the minute we get the camera pointed, people have more natural expressions. Don't bother to tell people, 'Say cheese,' or 'Smile,'" Ramiro says. "You smile; they smile. Your smile sets the subject up to relax, and the photos are more apt to be good ones."

4. Follow the action. This tip reminds photographers to move the camera to follow the action they want to catch: soccer players running, basketball players loping back and forth, children jumping rope, and so on. When we move the camera *with* the subject of our photo, we are more apt to get our subject *in* the picture frame and not end up with photos of miscellaneous arms, legs, and feet. Once children get this idea, they can move the camera smoothly to catch good action shots.

5. Look behind the subject before taking a picture. Ramiro says that many photographers are not aware of this tip, and as a result they photograph people with all kinds of things growing out of their heads: the plants or trees behind them, dog ears, table lamps, poles, bedposts, and so on. Ramiro also suggests that photographers make sure that the background is always darker than the subject of the photograph. He says a good check behind a subject's head is always worth the time.

6. Always use your flash outside. This strategy is possible with some cameras and not with others, but Ramiro feels that utilizing the outdoor flash provides consistently good photos outdoors. Without this suggestion, students who do not understand camera lighting misuse available outdoor light, and their photos do not turn out well. This tip gives children a chance to take outdoor shots successfully even if they have minimal knowledge of lighting. "Always look for some shade or overhang for your photograph," Ramiro advises, "not just bright sun."

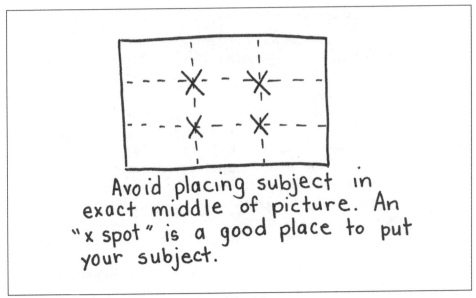

Figure 3–3. Diagram showing the "rule of thirds"

7. Avoid putting the subject in the exact middle of the picture frame. This tip is called the rule of thirds. (This tip is more helpful for my older students than my first graders.) To explain this stragtegy, Ramiro draws a rectangle and divides it into nine boxes (like a tick-tack-toe grid). He puts an X in the four corners of the center box. These places where the lines have an X are the best areas for putting the subject in any photograph. The exact middle space is *not* the best place to focus a picture. (See Figure 3–3.)

With older students, Ramiro pulls up photographs on the computer and shows the same photographs cropped different ways. Sometimes he shows the photo with the subject dead center (in the exact middle), which is *not* as effective as moving the lens over, up, or down to a place with an X. Showing kids different compositions of the same photo makes his point about the importance of putting the subject in the part of the picture frame indicated by an X in his drawing.

Although this information is too complex for my first graders (and I do not share it with them), they still get some wonderful pictures.

Ramiro's tips do help with photographic success, but I consider his final piece of advice to be most important of all for those of us working with photography in the classroom: "Give kids lots of opportunities and freedom to take photos. Show them how to be bold, and encourage them to *play* with what they are doing. Stress the fun and enjoyment of taking pictures."

What Photographic Equipment Do You Need in Your Classroom?

With countless types of photographic equipment available, it is important to know how to budget and choose well to get the most mileage in the classroom. Getting opinions from the staff at several stores' camera departments is helpful, as is checking with friends and colleagues. Articles in photography magazines can be useful. I am now much more enthused about digital cameras than the point-and-shoot film cameras I used to use. I would purchase inexpensive digital cameras and skip disposable cameras for home use if the budget were too tight for both types of cameras. I have found it important to have at least two digital cameras in the classroom because I want to be able to photograph children as they take pictures. I have also liked having a camera with a printer dock so that I can get immediate pictures without having to rely on my classroom computer and printer for photos. I also have an additional small photo printer that takes various memory cards. This combination works for me.

Although the most inexpensive Kodak EasyShare camera-and-dock duos are at the easy and beginner end of the camera spectrum, my students and I have gotten some terrific photos with this system. Several other companies now have similar cameras and printers that they sell as a package.

When I asked Ramiro for his suggestions for photographic equipment in the classroom, he had two recommendations. His first idea was to have four digital cameras and have students work in groups of five to take photos. Photos could then be downloaded to a computer using a card reader, which would also have to be purchased, as would a memory card for each camera. Ramiro's second suggestion, less costly, was to have two digital cameras with students working in groups of five, and while some of them photographed each other, the remaining students could download their photos to the computer via a card reader or use the memory card to make prints.

The main idea is to give students lots of opportunities to take pictures. Ramiro doesn't see this as a problem with younger children, but he has found it to be difficult to get middle school students to take pictures of each other. "If you can't take pictures of each other, how are you going to take pictures of other people?" he asks them.

Ramiro suggests hooking a laptop up to a projector so pictures can be shown large, for group viewing. "Critique is important after photos are taken," he says. "Kids need time to look at photos and analyze them, as well as process what was done well, what could have been done differently."

"It is important to get past hesitation," Ramiro says. "Take the picture! Otherwise you have no image."

In my classroom I have three digital cameras (with Marsha Oviatt's donation). Two of the cameras can make prints on the printer dock. I make prints from the third camera on the computer or on the small photo printer that takes memory cards.

One of my budgeting strategies is to watch for sales. As soon as new camera and printing equipment comes on the market, older items go on sale. I have three memory cards that I use on the photo dock and in the photo printer in the classroom.

How to Afford Camera Equipment

Two bottom-of-the-line digital cameras, purchased on sale, one or two card readers, possibly a camera printer dock or a small photo printer, and two memory cards, and you're set for the year. How to afford this? Here are some ideas:

- Write a small grant.
- Let everyone—family, friends, school and district personnel, parents of your students, and so on—know what you need. You may be surprised to find monetary support, or even the gift of unused camera equipment, printing cartridges, or printing paper. This information also helps out those who don't know what to get you for your birthday or Christmas.
- Ask your principal, district office, and district resource center, if there is one, about camera equipment. Perhaps there is equipment available, or even money in the budget.
- Ask about education and teacher discounts in camera stores and places where camera equipment is sold.
- Try the Internet—there are websites that match teachers with donors. Many classroom donor programs are listed at the American Federation of Teachers website: www.aft.org/teachers. Type in "donations."
- Try trading or selling unused camera equipment of your own for different items online.
- Purchase equipment with another teacher or with your grade level. Share your purchases and split the cost.

You can always start small and add items as you can afford them. A lot can be done with imagination and a single camera. As I mentioned in Chapter 1, most of my early photographic projects in the classroom were done with extremely minimal equipment.

4

Photography
A Way In for English Language Learners

You don't understand anything until you learn it more than one way.
—Marvin Minsky

Early in the school year, after I read my first graders *To Be a Kid* (Ajmera and Ivanko 1999), my group spontaneously began talking about what it was like to be a kid. The discussion was lively, and even children with little command of English made an effort to contribute. When I suggested that this was a topic they might want to write about, the kids were all for it—after all, as they knew, they were the experts. I gave them the option of using blank paper, lined paper, or sentence frame paper with a few lines, space to draw, and the words "To be a kid means _____." The children helped me decide on the sentence frame, taken right from the book, but they didn't have to use it. They could pick whatever paper felt most comfortable to work on.

During this writers workshop period, children could also continue working on writing in progress or pursue other topics. One of the results reminded me of the difficulties families—and children in school—face when they move to a new country and do not know the language. Children who chose the "to be a kid" topic came up with some interesting ideas, many of them what I would have expected: They wrote about playing soccer, going to the park, getting a dog, having fun with parents, brothers, and sisters, and so on. There was the literal child who wrote, "To be a kid means I em a kid." But the one that stopped me in my tracks spoke to me of some of the hidden challenges second language speakers face at home. José had written: "To be a kid means 'Help your Dad read English.'"

Many of my children do important jobs like this —translating for their parents —far beyond their ages and abilities. They help their families as they try to acquire a new language themselves and apply themselves to learn in that language in school.

Unfortunately, my students do not have much access to bilingual learning. I can help Spanish speakers, but I sometimes have as many as seven different languages spoken in the classroom. My solution for teaching this multilingual population is to *show* my students as much as I can as I speak. I use gestures, facial expressions, drawings and many visual aids. I have also found a new device to help me out: photography.

Photography as a Learning Tool

Photos stimulate a lot of language. They clarify a lot of language too. Everyone wants to be in photographs, take pictures, and talk about them. And the camera provides a new tool for children: another way for them to express themselves. It gives them a feeling of power and control over a piece of equipment, and that helps compensate for the lack of control they may feel over not yet speaking English. Photography gives my English language learners (ELLs) an additional language— another way for them to convey who they are and show what they know.

Like José, who couldn't speak much English when school started, kids can tell their stories with the photos they take. And when they get their pictures developed or printed, they can try to talk about them and write about them too. Since I feel immediacy is important here, I like having digital cameras with a photo dock or a photo printer—or a computer and printer—in order to process photos right away in the classroom. When there is no wait time, kids don't lose their impetus to communicate. I do not even attempt to make a photograph for all children at the same time so that everyone gets a new photo at once. Making one photo for a child who is ready for it is manageable. Over time, all children will have personal photos for their own collections. I also make photocopies of many pictures, especially good ones of more than one student. This helps keep the photography project going and reduces expense.

My friend Dr. Ryan James, who teaches English as a second language (ESL) classes at the university level in Budapest, built his entire course work around photos he has taken. His program, called *Photo Card Education Collection: Photos Included* (2004), uses his laminated 4- by 6-inch photographs to stimulate students to ask and answer questions, learn vocabulary, and practice descriptive language and sentence structure. Ryan took these photos in several different European countries, and his collection includes at least one picture for each class member to use. His classes focus on both individual and group work. He varies lessons by including generic questions and activities that could be used with any photo cards:

- Where do you think the photo was taken?
- What do you observe in the picture?
- What would the photograph say if anything in the picture could talk to you?

- What was this person doing right before (or after) this picture was taken?
- List nouns or verbs, words for texture, color words, and so on.

Ryan creates questions for music (students pretend the photo is a CD cover) and for literature (asking students to think of the photograph as a book cover and tell about the book) and uses any other links and details that individual photographs suggest.

In my own program I also use photographs to stimulate and encourage language. With permission, I use pictures of my students—all kinds of photos from our year together, as well as photos of former children in my classes. I use photos from some photography books (one copy for classroom use is permitted under copyright laws), and I get some photographs from Internet sites. With permission, I use photocopies of snapshots taken by students at home and on the playground, as well as in the classroom. Kids are propelled to talk about these photographs because they find them so exciting—naturally, because they, along with their friends and families, personally star in them! These pictures generate a lot of positive energy as well as language. And best of all, as Dr. Ryan James says, "Serious learning happens often when we incorporate fun. The more laughs, giggles, and tickles we create, the greater impression is being made and the more knowledge will be retained in students' memories" (2004, 1).

Creativity is an important aspect of using photos to elicit language. Kids enjoy coming up with the questions to use with pictures, such as What new playground game is this? What new toy did we invent? What math story problem does the picture show? and Which pictures can we put together to make a new story?

Photographs encourage students—and teachers—to let go and to be as inventive as possible. The more imaginative the responses and the more students play and open up, the less anxiety they will feel and the more their language will progress.

When my children use our photographs, they work individually or in small groups and then share, if they wish, in our large group to culminate the activity. First graders start out thinking in very literal ways but then loosen up and create their own stories. The sillier the stories, the more they enjoy the activity, and the more likely they are to clamor to talk, to take language to heart, and to use it mindfully. The kids also enjoy writing about the photographs, as they do with their own snapshots when they are working on their personal memory books and class stories. For more on these projects, see Chapters 2 and 8.

Photo Learning Center

I sometimes use this "tell about the photo" activity as a small-group learning center (see Chapter 8, "Imagination Stations"). I often make photocopies of photos to be used in this center, and this cuts photographic printing costs. Each group of four or five children selects the photo it wants to talk about. Creative drama can also be used with storytelling and photography. Sometimes my kids act out the photographs they have chosen. Lots of language results from these activities in small groups, as children help each other perform with words, gestures, and movement to express things they can't say in English. The photograph is a point of reference or sometimes just a good starting point for an activity. Kids find this to be a lot of fun.

Children can suggest ideas as well, and they even peruse photography books to come up with pictures, story ideas, or themes that interest them. I sometimes group kids with limited English with those who are more fluent. Other times, I put children of similar language capabilities in the same group. This latter grouping ensures that all students get the opportunity to talk and participate without being overshadowed by more fluent language speakers.

Frequently, these photo discussion and story sessions lead to the creation of class murals, charts, and big books. Kids love to create the things they have been talking about using paper scraps, crayons, pens, and other mixed media. When their art is complete, we often label it with their reflections and vocabulary words and put these pieces on the walls or bulletin boards. Students then have references to use all year as they develop their own vocabularies and stories. Their responses are often made within the language structure of a particular story, which helps ELLs find it easier to respond. And of course, kids are free to say things absolutely their own way.

For example, after we read *Moving Day*, by Robert Kalan (1996), a story about a hermit crab who was looking for the perfect shell, students created their own crab-and-shell artwork and came up with the words their hermit crab might have said: "This shell is too wobbly," "My shell is too bumpy," or "This polka dot shell looks silly." The cutout crab-and-shell drawings were affixed to craft sticks so the children could act out each hermit crab's complaint about its shell. When sticks were removed, the pasted-on crab-and-shell creations made a great mural. Excerpts from the kids' writing were enlarged and attached to the mural as well.

Individual puppet shows are a variation of this project. Keep the cutout drawings on the craft sticks and give children 12-by-18-inch pieces of construction paper to use to create their own settings. When the drawings are complete, I ask children to draw a light pencil line on this paper to show the path of the hermit crab or other main character. I then cut the path for them with a craft knife. Kids can act out their own stories by sticking the craft stick behind the paper and popping the puppet up in the front, where the action is!

Photocopied snapshots of the children may be cut out and attached to additional craft sticks to add interest and further dimension to the stories. The more freedom the students have, so they can be involved in this project in their own ways, the better!

Figure 4–1. Kids get very involved in Box Theatre plays.

Box Theatre Art

For another puppet activity, stand a cardboard box on its side with all four top flaps open. Kids can decorate the bottom (now the back of the box) and flaps with background scenes to create a theatre. Show children how to affix their own cutout photos to slices of paper towel rolls. These circular bases enable the photos to stand up. Kids can move these personal figures around to tell a story or perform a play. Recently our box theatre was a castle inhabited by a prince, a princess, a few cutout creatures, several monsters, and many first graders. Children did a lot of talking as they became involved in playing with this theatre. (See Figure 4–1.)

Photos may also be used to make individual masks or puppets. Although I have changed the craft slightly, the inspiration for this activity comes from the book *Puppet Mania*, by John Kennedy (2004). A copy paper–sized photograph is needed to make the photo puppet. I simply enlarge an existing photo or school picture to standard copy paper size, getting the biggest-possible photo of a child's head. I trim off any excess paper. Then I cut the face into two pieces, cutting all the way across the photo, right between the child's lips. I fold a simple piece of 6-by-6-inch red or

1. Cut out enlarged photocopy.

2. Cut photocopy through the lips. Cut under long hair, if necessary, to end up with top and bottom of face.

3. Cut "mouthpiece" of construction paper - mouth color of choice - about six inches long and width of face (or just width of mouth).
Fold in half.
Fold up one-half-inch flap at each end.

Fold

Folded-up flaps

4. Attach top piece of photo to top flap. Fasten behind top lip with glue stick or tape.

→ Flap. behind

Attach bottom lip to flap ↑

5. Squeeze and release paper to make photo talk.

← chin

6. To strengthen and "round" head, make one or two cuts.

Overlap. Glue or tape.

Figure 4–2. It's easy to make a photo puppet.

pink construction paper in half to create a mouth. I fold up the front and back edges of this paper one-half inch to create a flap. Then I affix the top part of the child's face photo to the top flap of the folded mouth, so that the paper is attached at the top lip, with the rest of the photo above it. (I use glue or tape behind the photocopy.) I attach the second half of the photo paper so that it hangs below the bottom mouth flap. Squeeze and release the construction paper "mouth" to open and close and make the puppet "talk." See Figure 4–2 for illustrated instructions for making this craft.

As simple as these puppets are, the children find them very believable. When I experimented to make the first one, using the photo of a child who had moved away, my kids were ecstatic. "Oh, there's Nathan!" they said, and they began talking to the puppet. I took a one-inch cut in Nathan's chin, overlapped it, and taped it at the back so the face would be slightly rounded. Then I left the puppet attached to the whiteboard with a magnet while we went on with learning centers. A few minutes later I came upon a child chatting away to "Nathan." Turning, she explained to me, "We haven't seen Nathan in such a long time."

These simple yet heartfelt responses made me decide that this project was a go.

Children's Books Are Great Resources for Language and Imagination!

One of my favorite ways to work with English learners is to share children's literature books and work on follow-up art activities that grow out of the kids' story responses. If ELLs are really involved with the story, language just flows and so do ideas. My first graders started making excited verbal comments about Jane Yolen's book *How Does a Dinosaur Say Good Night?* (2003) even before I finished reading it aloud! After I read the book, they created their *own* literary version: *How Does a Dinosaur Play with Me?* We then enjoyed a new Jane Yolen release, *How Do Dinosaurs Play with Their Friends?* (2006). Each child made a dinosaur using pens, glue sticks, and scraps of colored paper. Kids stuck their creatures on the mural using rolls of tape or glue sticks. Then they added their personal cutout photos to the mural in such a way as to make their own dinosaurs interact with their photographs. The class as a group then had fun helping create the names of games the dinosaurs played with our class. Some of my favorite invented kid-and-dinosaur activities were Throw the Kid in the Hoop (Jacelynn is tossed up into a basketball hoop by her dinosaur) and Be My Snack (Lupita, clutched in the grasp of her dinosaur, is about to become her creature's lunch). The name of Edward's game was Slide the Dinosaur Down, and he placed his photo on the dinosaur's neck.

Participation books, with a repeating refrain, are great to extend this type of activity, as are poems and songs we have learned. We actually used the tune of the old song "There's a Spider on the Floor" to create our own lyrics for the dinosaur mural, with one verse for each child. For example, using the pattern of the song, we sang, "Slide Edward down its neck, down its neck. Slide Edward down its neck, down its neck. Who can ask for anything more, than a slide down a dinosaur? Slide Edward down its neck, down its neck!" If you don't know the song, written by Tom Paxton, it is available on several tapes, including one by Raffi. (There is a book written by Raffi in the Raffi Songs to Read series titled *Spider on the Floor* [1996].) You can also put the lyrics to your own music or chant them as a group.

Most of the words to our songs don't rhyme at all, but that doesn't stop us from singing them, enjoying them, getting meaningful language practice, and having a great old time!

Big Books

Big books are a logical step for using photos in the classroom. We work on a lot of skills as we make books, and kids can't wait to read them. This gets in a lot of reading and language practice in ways that make sense to children who don't speak or understand much English. Other kids get a lot out of the activity, too. Here is a list of some big books I have made using photography in my classroom:

Big Book of the Alphabet Kids use some photos, augmented by magazine cutouts and drawings, and put together an illustrated page, with objects labeled, for each letter of the alphabet. One photo on each page features kids in class whose names begin with the targeted letter.

The Big Book of Alphabet Photos This project is reminiscent of a wonderful concept book, *Arlene Alda's ABC: What Do You See?* (2002). Photographs in this picture book, when looked at closely, resemble letters of the alphabet: a curled pink shrimp forms a *c*; the letter *x* is created by the way trunks of two trees curve around each other; and B is a cleverly cut apple slice. This is a sophisticated book, and it would take a lot of work to create a similar big book in class. But the process does develop the seeing eye. Alda has a related book about numbers: *Arlene Alda's 1 2 3* (2004). Although I haven't taken the time to create a complete big book like this with students, we do identify letters in this way and take some photos when we take an alphabet walk.

One easy way to do this kind of book would be to have multiple cameras (digital or disposable) and let children work on assignment in small groups. Each group would be responsible for photos to represent specific letters or numbers. There would be a lot of surprises if we worked as a team to put this type of book together!

The Big Book of Room 7 Superstars This book devotes a page to each of the children in my class. We have created several of these books in different ways. One type of book has a photo of the child at the top and then shared writing text about the student (written by the whole class). The information on this page can be about a child's family, likes and dislikes, special interests, and so on. The text is dependent upon what the students want to share and the interview questions the class asks.

Who ARE You?   This is one of my favorite big books. Much like the previous photo idea, each child is photographed doing a special activity of choice, real or imaginary. Children come up and tell me their brief stories at the computer. This text is added to the child's page with the cutout photo and drawing. For example, Luis' page shows him touching the ground, with a football (cut out of a magazine) in front of him and all kinds of drawings of dogs and turtles on the 50-yard line. His text reads, "I am playing football. I am a football star. I am the Quarterback. By Luis."

In this big book, children are doing all manner of fantastic things that are great fun to read about. We admire the photo collage artwork, too. Last year's book shows, among other things, a child sitting on a crocodile and children riding in a rocket ship, in a plane, on a magic carpet, on a horse, and on a flying leopard. One is at the beach; others are on stage, at the zoo, or involved with monsters in a variety of different ways. I particularly enjoy Aryanna's entry: Her cutout photo shows her lying down on her drawing of a fancy bed. "They call me Sleeping Beauty," she says. "They call me that because I sleep."

This particular book was so popular that I reduced it and gave each child an 8½-by-11-inch photocopied version to keep. The kids love to read this at home.

The Big Book of Butterflies   This big book shares our photos and writing about caterpillars, chrysalides, and finally, butterflies. It shows children studying each stage of the metamorphosis and then releasing butterflies in our school garden. It also features Daniel, after the butterfly release, hanging upside down from the playground equipment "to see what it was like to be a chrysalis."

South San Francisco, Then and Now   This book has student-drawn maps and drawings of the city and photos taken in the past (copies from the historical society) and in the present (taken by my students). Original writing and collages are included as well. We have done several social studies projects about our town, and we put this book together to celebrate the upcoming city centennial, which takes place in 2008 (see Chapters 5 and 7).

The Big Book of Opposites   We brainstorm words for opposites. There is a lot of vocabulary development here, and photos support comprehension. We take pictures of kids "near and far," "up and down" (on the playground equipment is the most fun), "over and under," "happy and sad," and so on. My dear friend Kristi Yee creates a similar small class book in her kindergarten classroom. I especially love her pages for "asleep and awake": photos show her principal, Tim Sullivan, at his desk, acting out both words. Of course, the picture of the principal sleeping with his head on his desk is her students' favorite photo in the book!

The Big Book of Riddles Before we make this one, we read a lot of riddle books together. We practice telling riddles too.

The Book of Rhyming Words This book is similarly fun to create. Before we begin, I especially like to share Bruce McMillan's picture books *Puffins Climb, Penguins Rhyme* (2001), *One Sun: A Book of Terse Verse* (1992), and *Puniddles* (1982). These are illustrated with McMillan's photos.

I Spy We make our own "I spy" habitat in a large area on the classroom rug, using big blocks and all kinds of small items just waiting to be found. This project falls down a few times as we create it, but the kids are very careful. I help add the small items, such as tiny toys, alphabet letters, buttons, and so on. When we photograph different parts of this scene, we have the visuals we need to create several different pages of a big book. We use the I Spy books of Jean Marzollo and Walter Wick (e.g., 1995) as a model for our own books. Kids also love to make lists of different items they can find in the scene. To complicate matters for them, I always add several more small items after school.

We also make many books for other curriculum areas, such as math big books with photo story problems, graphs and fractions, photos to illustrate different math facts, and so on. Children love to take their own photos and write their story problems. These can be real puzzles.

Big books are great for English learners as well as for the rest of the class. They are a place to showcase our writing, our photos, and our art, and they are great for practicing reading individually, in small groups, and all together. The kids love them!

Some big books are later made into charts. These can be hung up for reference and help kids with vocabulary development, math, and tricky concepts.

Vocabulary Development

Kids' creations with writing, drawings, cutout photos, and sketched scenes hang all over our classroom. These are great to pull from to make vocabulary development charts, as mentioned earlier. For example, I asked the children to come up with sentences for a photo chart using action words or verbs. The resulting chart extended their vocabularies, and they had a good time making it. Some of my favorite sentences, mounted on a chart with corresponding photos and art, were

Hanchong and Sagar <u>fly</u> over the jungle.

Luis <u>throws</u> the football to Marlo.
Edward <u>slides</u> down the dinosaur.
Angelina <u>rides</u> a horse to school.

The kids love to see themselves starring in the action word chart, and it's a good reference for spellings of names as well as the emphasis on verbs. Later on, we will put a different-colored line under the nouns in each sentence to further extend the chart's use. Every child wants to be represented. With a digital camera and photo dock and printer available, this is easy to do, although I do use little group photos of three or four children to illustrate some of the sentences (rather than use photos of individual students). This cuts down on the number of photos that need to be taken.

Vocabulary Word Parade

"A vocabulary parade is so you learn lotsa good new words to use and you put 'em on a hat. It's fun, too, and silly." This is how my students describe one of our vocabulary activities.

When I saw the kids' reaction to Debra Frasier's picture book *Miss Alaineous: A Vocabulary Disaster* (2007), I knew we were going to have our *own* vocabulary parade, just like the fifth graders in the story. While Frasier's characters came to school in full costume, our costumes were easy and quick to make: vocabulary word hats. All we needed were paper-strip headbands, tongue depressors, drawing implements, tape, a stapler, and imagination.

The first task was to come up with interesting words. For our preliminary venture into the vocabulary parade business, we didn't restrict ourselves to themes, just to words we liked. The children called out special words, and I quickly wrote them down on large pieces of easel-sized paper. When we ran out of thoughts, we looked through our school newspapers (see Chapter 6) and got word ideas there from stories we had previously written: *performer, tightrope walker, photographers, firefighter,* and so on. A wonderful book to help us jump-start our creativity was *Brian Wildsmith's Amazing World of Words* (1997). The picture book has words and pictures for several different habitats and themes. But before we used other resources, the children used their own interests and imaginations, and we filled up two large papers with *their* ideas.

Now the fun began: Each child chose a special word to illustrate, print, practice reading and writing, and learn. We had action words like *erupting volcano,* as well as such favorite nouns as *dinosaurs, sports cars,* and even *ballet folklórico* (no surprise since we had just seen a performance the day before). Each child easily chose a particular word and illustrated it on white construction paper with marking pens. Illustrations were cut out, words were printed on tag board sentence strips, and then

Name Moises

We made hats tey wer wrds on the hats my wrd was Inventor It was fun to make hats tetor made a hat to tetor tuke a picktor of us wering or hats tey wer a lote of Wrds

Figure 4–3. New words are fun to learn with a volcabulary parade!

these marvels were assembled. I made a headband for each student using manila tag board sentence strips, and I helped staple the cutout illustration to the front of each band. We taped a tongue depressor behind this, again at the front of each headband, and attached the child's word to the top of that. When looking at each student, we could see the illustration on the headband and the word poised on the tongue depressor above the picture. These were quick and easy costumes, and they were fun to read! See Figure 4–3 for a look at our vocabulary-smart kids!

Since categorization is a skill we need to practice, we worked hard to decide on categories for our words and grouped children accordingly. I took a picture of each group. Some of our categories were living creatures (although we put *dinosaur* in this group by mistake); cars and trucks and things that go; performers; places; and people. (We had just been on a Science Circus field trip.) Since we couldn't figure out how to categorize *flags of countries* and *erupting volcano*, our last category was miscellaneous. I printed out our group photos and then enlarged them to ledger size on the school copy machine. We turned these pictures into a mural, adding on many strips of other words we wanted to learn. We also made a class big book, *Our Vocabulary Parade!*

Photo Poetry

Each year we create a class poetry book as a culmination of a year of learning favorite poems. This also becomes a class yearbook. Children each choose a poem from those we have memorized, act it out, and get their photo taken by me as they pose. They then incorporate the cutout photo with a drawing to illustrate the poem. One of my favorite poetry book pages last year featured Hanchong riding a dragon. He used his cutout photo, a felt pen dragon drawing, and a traditional Chinese Mother Goose nursery rhyme:

> The sun comes up
> > like red fire
> I follow my friend
> > through the skies.
> He thinks his horse
> > is quick,
> But the dragon I ride
> > is as swift as the wind.
> —*Translation by Sharon Hui Ng*

We enjoy the poetry collection compiled by Robert Wyndham, *Chinese Mother Goose Rhymes* (1998). Another favorite page in our class poetry book featured Jacelynn. Her picture was used several times, reduced to different sizes to show perspective and to pinpoint the fact that she was flying away. My poem was illustrated with her photos; the largest photo was in the foreground by a line drawing of a house, and cutout photos grew smaller as they receded over the hills and clouds in the distance:

> The wind blows high,
> The wind blows low,
> Out the window,
> And away I go. . . .
> —*Pat Barrett Dragan*

I am rainbow.
I am sun.
I am homes.
But the wind blows.
And wind is mad.
—by Alex Fregoso

Figure 4–4. Alex writes a poem and illustrates it with a photo collage.

Last year I was delighted to find that children used some of their own photography—snapshots taken at home or at school—to illustrate their poems. Luis chose the traditional rhyme "This is the day they give babies away" and illustrated it with a photo his mom had taken of him teaching his baby brother to write on an easel. He had drawn a big sign next to his brother that said, "Babies are free!" Leslie and her baby brother read together in the photographic collage illustrating her chosen poem, my adaptation of "The More We Get Together": "The more we read together, the happier we'll be!" (Dragan 2001).

First-Grade Poets

As a related project, we frequently write our own poetry, and I type it so that the children get professional-looking copies in final form. Sometimes these personal poems are illustrated with collage: photos, magazine cutouts, paper scraps, and children's drawings. The paper I give each child has an "art square" of about six inches by six inches. It has room for the printed poem below it. Children use the art square spaces to create special illustrations for their own poems.

Alex wrote the following poem. Like many poems young children write, it didn't look like much until it was typed and presented as a finished piece of literature. I was stunned as I listened to Alex read it. I was even more moved when I saw what he did with his collage illustration (see Figure 4–4). Bits and pieces of torn tree photographs surround his own reflective photo, placed in the bottom portion of his drawing. Oil pastels detail the path and havoc of the wind. Alex's collage mirrors so well the words and the flow of his poem.

> I am rainbow.
> I am sun.
> I am homes.
> But the wind blows.
> And wind is mad.

I am so glad to have heard Alex read his poem. Now when I read it, his is the voice I hear.

Regie Routman has some wonderful books about teaching children to write poetry (see her series Kids' Poems, e.g., 2000). She has a book for each grade level, K–4. I particularly enjoy the way the illustrations show handwritten drafts of children's poems juxtaposed with the final typed versions of their writing.

Some of the work the children have done with photography and language arts reminds me that we need to practice, experiment, and try things out in our teaching also, rather than dismiss too soon our own rough drafts and half-conjured ideas.

5

Photography Across the Curriculum

Happiness . . .
It lies in the joy of achievement,
In the thrill of creative effort.
—Vincent van Gogh

 Use of cameras enriches curriculum across the board in our classroom: in the arts, sciences, math, reading, language arts, and language acquisition, as well as physical education. It's great to look around and see positive photos of our class members everywhere. This chapter includes a sampling of additional ways my students and I have used cameras and photographs to make amazing discoveries, create astounding things, and enjoy learning to the fullest.

My friend Dr. John Becker tells me that the word *photography* literally means "writing with light." What a great image! I find this to be very close to the word *enlighten*. This pleases me because much of what we do with photos clarifies, enriches, enlivens, and enlightens our studies in every area of the curriculum.

Our latest interest—close-up photography—started when Edward brought me a flower: a beautiful, full red rose. It was slightly crooked on its short stem and unusual in the way it had opened up, partly wide open, other places tight with smooth surfaces and some deep shadows. My first graders and I enjoyed looking at it and talking about it as I hunted up a small vase. "I wonder what it would look like deep down inside there," I mused.

"You'd have to really ask a bee," said Eliana.

Another child suggested we take a photo of the flower up close, and then "grow it" on the copy machine. "We could paste pictures of us shrunk little all over the big flower picture," Dariana said. I could just see this image as she spoke: a giant flower photocopy with tiny cutout photos of children and their teacher glued on. My kids were all for the idea, and several said this would make a great collage and a good story. Aryanna said she wished we could have a flower adventure like the trips kids take in the Magic School Bus books. In Joanna Cole's picture books, such as *The Magic School Bus: Inside the Earth* (1989), students and their teacher travel in depth to different places to learn. My class liked the idea of creating our own flower trip story as a group and writing it down. After talking over the idea, the children decided that they needed to know more about flowers before they could write this story. We planned to get some books from the library and help this spark of an idea to grow.

Our group flower fantasy trip brought other ideas to mind for me to do before the end of the term: I made a note to myself to teach some art lessons about Georgia O'Keeffe and her beautiful gigantic flower paintings and to give the kids additional opportunities to express themselves through watercolors and oil pastels. Another idea, and one I acted on right away, was to show my first graders how to take close-ups with one of the digital cameras. This was a big hit! Two or three kids took photos of Edward's flower with a close-up lens. The class was amazed at the detail that could be seen when the photos were printed out.

After almost a year of photography activities and related aesthetic experiences, my children are thinking like artists, scientists, and writers. And now that they realize more of the digital camera's capabilities, they have a new interest in photographing close-ups.

On a short walk to the dell, a small, secluded open area adjacent to our school grounds, the kids take intense notice of flowers, trees, grass, and birds and strive to use both the built-in telephoto lens and the close-up lens to get some photos. These photographs, they say, will help them to "really look at things and learn stuff."

This new interest in close-ups coincides with the arrival of our five painted lady caterpillars—the main event in our butterfly unit. We watch these creatures change and grow over an eight-week period. Since some things happen fast and are difficult to see in a classroom of twenty children taking turns, occasional close-up photographs give everybody a better chance to note what is happening. The photos also document, scientifically, changes going on with these caterpillars. This is a real opportunity for my students to visualize science. (See Figure 5–1.)

Children continue to draw and write in their science journals. We take frequent caterpillar, chrysalis, and ultimately, butterfly photos, and line them up sequentially to get the big picture.

With more technological knowledge and equipment, children could take time-sequenced photographs of the caterpillars. In their book *Teaching with Digital Images*, editors Glen Bull and Lynn Bell (2005) detail ways to use time-lapse photography to catch events and record them for further observation and analysis.

Bull and Bell suggest that this project is more appropriate for older students. The device they use to capture images at regular intervals over several hours is a QX3 digital microscope. Another possibility is to use a digital camera with a built-in time-lapse mode setting. According to Bull and Bell, there is also camera software, called

Figure 5–1. Butterfly science.

CameraScope, available for free download at www.teacherlink.org/tools. CameraScope is a visualizaion tool that helps students observe events that are too small, happen too fast or too slow. It manages and displays images.

Science concepts are enriched by use of the camera. When we get a new betta fish, some children choose to photograph the steps to set up the aquarium. Other students write about setting up the fish tank, and one child, Andrea, reminds them that they need to write about things in order or the story won't make sense.

Here are some other photos children have taken to illuminate science curriculum:

- a series of photos of changes as our crystal garden grows
- photos to show the life of Crab Louie, our hermit crab
- changes in local trees throughout the seasons
- a series of photos of our ant farm to document the development of tunnels
- a sequence of photos showing the growth of plants
- before and after photos of the growth of kids, shown standing next to an enlarged yardstick

- examples of our changing weather
- a series of photos about different types of clouds

The Life of a Rose

Edward, the child who brought the rose to school, seemed very interested in sequence when he talked about his flower. I listened to him chat with several children about his experiences: how he saw the rose grow when he helped work in the garden, how his mom picked it, and why he decided to bring the flower to school: "It got really red and big." Edward's attachment to his flower reminded me of Antoine de Saint-Exupery's character, the Little Prince, in the classic book of the same name (2003). I gave Edward a large piece of drawing paper folded in four parts. In each numbered section he drew and wrote about his rose, from the time it grew in his yard until his mother picked it and he brought it to school. He added a photograph to the fourth box: his own picture in the classroom, smelling the flower. (See Figure 5–2.)

After seeing Edward's work, several other children were inspired to make sequential drawing and writing projects incorporating a personal photograph. When we shared these with our fifth-grade book buddies, we learned that they had been using photos to make sequential projects of their own: personal time lines.

The Time of Your Life!

Jocelyn Berke, a fifth-grade teacher, had taught a unit she called "The Time of Your Life!" She asked her students to use some personal photographs to illustrate important events in their own lives. They organized their photographs on 8½-by-44-inch paper (four pieced-together sheets of copy paper). They drew time lines, added dates, and filled in brief information about selected moments they wanted to highlight. Most children chose a new-baby picture to emphasize the day they were born. Many of the time lines included important events with siblings, parents, and extended family. Some work showed pictures taken in other countries, as well as some culturally diverse experiences students had before moving to the United States. Other time lines focused on graduation from kindergarten, riding a pony, special events with close friends. My kids were fascinated with these vignettes of other children's lives.

Nature Studies

My colleague Rebecca Fishman engages her third graders in writing reports on the computer. Her students take many photographs on nature study field trips: pictures

Figure 5–2. Edward creates a photo sequence chart about his rose.

of rare wildflowers and animals on San Bruno Mountain, all kinds of birds in the wetlands adjacent to San Francisco Bay, and sea creatures discovered in tide pools at the Fitzgerald Marine Reserve in Moss Beach, California. The students learn patience as they sit quietly to observe tide pools and watch animals emerge from their hiding places and resume their activities. Watching the elephant seals at nearby Año Nuevo Beach is another favorite study activity for our third graders.

Rebecca takes her students to the computer lab (available in our school for older students) and shows them how to download their digital photographs onto the computer and then place their photos in their reports. They also find related photographs on the Internet. The resulting work is very impressive and exciting to see. Real images play such a part in children's lives. Students need opportunities to become visually literate in the highly visual world we live in.

Storytelling and Visual Literacy

When I work on visual literacy experiences with my classes, both first graders and the after-school upper-grade students, I like to share images of fine arts. Students benefit a great deal from the opportunity to experience high-quality paintings, sculptures, architecture, and photographs and talk about them. These lessons benefit not only English language learners but also all students.

The National Gallery of Art, like many large prestigious museums, has educational websites. See the aforementioned resource book *Teaching with Digital Images* (Bull and Bell 2005) for further information. Following are some of the websites listed in this guide to obtain educational images:

National Gallery of Art (www.nga.gov): This website has a wide variety of digital images and teaching resources for K–12 teachers.

National Gallery of Art Classroom (www.nga.gov/education/classroom): The classroom is the main website for teachers who are working to integrate the arts into curriculum. It includes lessons for teachers and interactive experiences for students. Resources are listed by curriculum topic, art subject, or the artist's name.

NGA Kids(www.nga.gov/kids/kids.htm): This website is for children. It includes interactive art projects, such as online portraits and collage projects. See *Teaching with Digital Images* (Bull and Bell 2005) for more information about incorporating imagery into instruction.

Melding Art and Photography: Becoming Part of a Painting

I find that art prints and transparencies of art reproductions are a great way to teach art history and make it relevant to children. These lessons help students learn to look critically at pieces of art and talk about what they observe. I like to take these art studies further by inviting my kids to become part of the painting or other work of art being discussed.

One way to do this is to make a transparency of an art print. I select the piece of art (often children make choices) and take the book to a copy shop. I ask to have one transparency made for classroom use, as is permitted under copyright regulations. When the transparency is shown on an overhead projector, it can be projected in varied sizes on a wall, whiteboard, or piece of butcher paper. Students enjoy talking about the art, pointing to details with a "magic brush" (a dry paintbrush), and showing their own pathways into to the painting. Best of all, they love to invent ways to pose in front of the picture and become part of it. Other children may sketch as a classmate mimes a dance with Degas' ballerinas, plays an old-fashioned game in front of the projection of Winslow Homer's *Snap the Whip*, or scrambles to pick up candy and treats as part of Diego Rivera's painting, *Piñata*. We take photos of children interacting with art in this way. These theatre art pictures are fascinating to look at. Recently my first graders became interested in early cave art. One of their ideas was to pretend to be drawing on a cave wall with a hunk of charcoal. Children took turns drawing cave images on an overhead transparency projection of cave art, and later on brown, crumpled packing paper or flattened-out paper bags.

To teach similar lessons involving children with fine arts, it is important to have easy access to some art prints or transparencies. I use both of these learning tools. I like prints because they can stay up in the classroom, and we can experience living with great pieces of art over time. (See the "References and Resources" section for suggestions on art print resources.) I like art transparencies because they can be projected large or small, and we can write on them, on the paper where they are being projected, or on blank acetates protecting the images. There is certain magic in turning on a machine and making these images appear. As a follow-up to an art history lesson, I often set out a number of prints to give children visual stimulation. They are free to draw or paint in the style of Monet, Klee, Matisse, Jacob Lawrence, or any other artist or combination of styles, and best of all, their own unique styles. In a related lesson, children may add a cutout photo of themselves to their artwork. In this way, they may photographically become part of *their* rendition of Jacob Lawrence's *Children at Play* or place their cutout photos of themselves *on their own paintings* of the bridge at Giverny, so they appear to be looking down at Monet-style water lilies. Another way to play and innovate with children's acetate photos and art transparencies is to place a clear acetate with a child's photo on it *over* the transparency of a piece of art. In this way, children can join in many scenes to become part of famous paintings.

Sometimes children will be so taken with a piece of art that they spontaneously act it out. I captured a group of three little girls on camera as they admired a classmate's new space in her mouth where her tooth had been—very like Norman Rockwell's work *Checkup*, also known as *The Lost Tooth*.

Enlarged photos of children in class, blown up on the copy machine or projected as overhead transparencies, are another way to provide interesting images to stimulate art, oral language, and writing.

Children learn a lot about art as they interact with transparencies and art prints and spend time creating their own artistic works. Collage—using some pieces in the style of specific artists along with personal photos, paint, and pasted-on papers—is another way to extend art history and photographic experiences. And the reflections kids write about artists, as well as about their own art, convey many details and a lot of learning. See the "References and Resources" section for some picture books to use with this type of lesson.

Social Studies and Photographs

In a similar bent, we use photos we have taken to create works in collage, murals, and personal writing in the area of social studies. Our digital cameras (and leftover disposable cameras) get heavy-duty usage on our field trips (see Chapter 7). The cameras provided children with comparative images of South San Francisco, some of which they photographed themselves. We also obtained copies of photos of the city one hundred years ago from the historical society. These resulting then-and-now shots were the impetus for my students' creation of a piece of art showing life in the city over more than a century. Based on their knowledge of South San Francisco today and what it was like in the past, children made a three-part mural: South San Francisco one hundred years ago, in the present, and in the year 2108.

First, we took another look at photos of the town as it was one hundred years ago. We looked at current-day photos we had taken and compared similarities and differences, then and now. We recorded our findings on sheets of easel-sized paper. Then we brainstormed to think of advances and changes the children might see if they could look into the future one hundred years from now. We asked analytical questions: How will people get around? Will they still use cars? Will other inventions help people get from one place to another? We used multimedia and a long piece of colored butcher paper for our masterpiece: We chose some copies of photos of South San Francisco that we had taken and used crayons, paper scraps, and marking pens to add further details. The three parts of the mural were done as a time line, in sequence: "Then," "Now," and "One Hundred Years from Now." When we were finished, the children talked about their creation. I typed up their ideas and reflections and attached them to their mural. And I wondered how many of the children would be living in South San Francisco to see the changes in the city fifty or even a hundred years from now.

I saved the mural for community art displays in public buildings—part of the South San Francisco centennial celebration in 2008.

Photographing a Math Problem

Children use cameras in math in many ways, mostly by thinking up a mathematical story, taking a picture of it, and writing the story problem. My students love to share these. We all had a fine time with Angelina's pet mice (fortunately made of plastic, but unfortunately ugly!), which she brought to use in her math problem. After moving them around a lot (they kept appearing and reappearing in unusual places in the classroom!), Angelina wrote a math problem about ears on mice. She lined up four of her mice, thought about their ears, and wrote: $2 + 2 + 2 + 2 = 8$. Then she wrote the story of her mice. (See Figure 5–3.)

Litzi used photos to make a fraction chart. She glued nine photos of kids' heads (photocopied and cut from the class picture) to a piece of paper. These were lined up in three rows, three heads to a row. In the bottom row, Litzi circled pictures of three children and wrote the fraction $1/3$ and the words *one third*. These visuals helped Litzi and her classmates understand a difficult concept.

Figure 5–3. Angelina creates a mice math problem.

Moises also used a photocopy of the class picture. He made a graph showing choices of favorite foods, using kids' heads to fill it in. Six glued-on photos of heads showed those who love tacos, ten heads showed pizza lovers, and four heads filled in the row for kids who like hamburgers best.

The kids like to work out math problems to go with photographs. This is a good small-group activity or learning center. These math pages can be turned into great big books, too.

Making Books

One of the most exciting uses of photographs across the curriculum has been incorporating them in our own reading materials by creating small books (four inches by six inches) and tiny books (two inches by two inches). I learned of this idea through the book *Real ePublishing, Really Publishing! How to Create Digital Books by and for All Ages* (Condon and McGuffee 2001). This book, as advertised, helps transform our classroom into our own publishing center. We create our own text on the computer and illustrate it with our own digital photography, just

63

moving the photographs onto the pages with the text we have written. Photos and text run back-to-back so paper is not wasted. It is a simple matter to cut the finished pages in half (or smaller, if a tiny book is being printed) and staple them.

Our first endeavor was to write a group book—through shared writing at the easel—about Hector and his father and the classroom visit (see Chapter 1 for more information). We called the book *Our Balloon Man*, and it featured actual photographs of Mr. León's balloon-making performance and snapshots of Hector and his classmates helping Mr. Léon create balloon flowers, animals, hats, and magic wands.

The RealeBooks' bookmaking template may be downloaded online. For more information about new software applications for Mac and Windows go to the website www.realebooks.com. When we work on a group book, we choose photos (four is a good number to start), and I make them into overhead transparencies. I place these transparencies on the projector, and the kids and I play with these images—and with language as well—as we look at the pictures projected on the screen, whiteboard, or white butcher paper. We move the transparencies around, think about our story, and decide which pictures would work best for front and back covers, as well as inside text.

As children come up with the book title and a sentence or two for each page, I jot down their words on a piece of acetate with an overhead pen. We reread our text, making changes and reordering words and pictures. As students become more familiar with this process, we can make longer books together.

Letting Kids Loose at the Overhead Projector

My class loves to take turns at the overhead projector in small groups of three or four, putting the book in order, rewriting text, including some extra photo acetates, and so on (see Figure 5–4). This is a worthwhile center.

When we have decided on the order of our text and photographs, I bring up the RealeBooks link on the computer—the template for making small books—and print copies of the books. My kids are always beside themselves with excitement and can't wait to read these and talk about them. We can make individual student books and small-group books as well as whole-group publications. (See Figure 5–5.)

Other photographic projects, including prints, books, and photo sharing, may be done on Scholastic's Shutterfly website: www.shutterfly.com/info/scholasticschool.jps. These are more polished books with actual covers, and they are more expensive. It is worth checking out this website to print and store photos and create single copies of class yearbooks or other photographic books for the classroom.

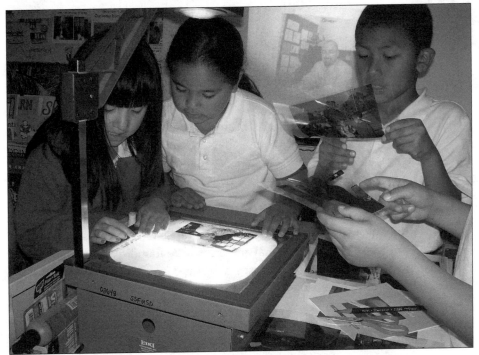

Figure 5–4. Children collaborate on a story on the overhead projector.

Hector and his dad are a good team!

Figure 5–5. Sample page from our web book *Our Balloon Man*.

A Sampling of Other Uses of Photos

Photos may be used at school in a myriad of other ways. Here is a small list to generate further ideas:

- Classroom organization photos: Pictures to place on cubbyholes, desks, and seating charts, job charts, class calendars, birthday charts, class rules chart
- Teacher records: Photos of bulletin boards and murals; writing and art samples and other lessons across the curriculum
- Photos of art for displays and exhibits
- Substitute information: Brief notes about important information for your substitute folder, supplemented with photographs (Now items such as homework and lunch tickets may more easily be found. A substitute can read notes and look at photos to see how our day goes. These notes could also be written by students.)
- Classroom observations and teacher reflections: Photos of children at work and play; annotated teacher comments
- Charts: Photographic reminders of procedures and strategies, such as ways to solve playground conflicts, how to stand up for yourself, how to glue, where to put things in the classroom
- Directions: How to play an outdoor game or a board game
- Science concepts: Scientific changes in a leaf, changes in the seasons; sequence photos of ice melting, clouds changing, plants and children growing, a crystal garden taking form, shadows shrinking and lengthening
- How-to photos: How to measure with a ruler or yardstick, mix paints, read with a buddy, make a friend
- Photos to record events and places, field trips and assemblies, classroom speakers and interviews
- Photocopied sample work: Classroom or individual books and stories, memory books, and albums
- Classroom images to further learning across the curriculum
- Photos to enhance self-esteem, show exemplary behavior and ideas
- Big books
- Photos to stimulate writing, create a bridge to writing
- Math story problems
- Photos to illuminate math concepts: graphs, patterns, math facts, shapes
- Photos for parent newsletters, school newspapers, classroom stationery, personalized cards, certificates of achievement
- Photo matching games, such as matching children's photos with their home address and phone number
- Photo face puzzles: Large cut-up photocopies of children's faces

- Photos of large class projects: An "I spy" habitat (see Chapter 4), castle or dinosaur scene, city of the future

In essence, I try to think of any curriculum I'm teaching in terms of photography. Odds are that the children and I will find a way to use photos to help make our studies easily understood, relevant to our lives, and fun to learn.

6

The Kids' Press
Kids Deliver the News

*The kids in our school are super excited when they see our newspaper
'cause they want to read it and find out what's going on and who's in it.*
—Sagar, first-grade photographer and reporter

"Hot off the press!" my first graders say every Friday, when we all trek to the office to deliver the current edition of our class-produced school newspaper. A monitor holds open the door, and two or three photographers of the week carry the ledger-sized page into the office and announce our arrival.

Usually our principal, Mario Penman, is on hand to peruse the new edition of the *Room 7 School Newspaper* and give my class positive feedback. When we delivered the first or second issue back in September, Mario asked the kids, "Who are the photographers?" Their names were listed under the photos, but he wanted to be sure to credit the children individually. "Luis and Hanchong this week," answered my students, "but we're *all* reporters!" (See Figure 6–1.)

Our secretary, Colleen Morello, always tapes the newspaper inside the office window so passersby can easily read it. I frequently see students, parents, and school personnel standing there to examine our work.

Over the evolution of this newspaper project, tackled once a week throughout the school year, the children *do* grow to think of themselves as reporters. They rev up their curiosity to write down their individual story ideas (we have a quickwrite early in the week), make whole-group topic lists at meetings on the rug, and keep a running tally of events and ideas to cover, to learn about, and to write about. We keep these ideas constantly within view on a large easel tablet, so that we can add to them, change and modify them, as well as delete those topics that don't meet our standards. We want subjects of schoolwide interest, featuring at least one Martin School student. Sometimes we write about school staff members and little-known facts about their work. Often our focus is on special school events. At least every other issue includes photographs of children in our class.

Our newspaper project promotes what Frank Smith calls "creating the urge to

Figure 6–1. Our newspaper delivery to the office.

know." As he explains in his book *Insult to Intelligence*, "Knowledge has to be sucked into the brain, not pushed into the brain. First you have to create a state of mind which craves knowledge" (1986).

At the beginning of the year our editions are done on 8½-by-11-inch paper with one story and photo, but as kids sharpen their skills and become more comfortable with how to create their own newspaper, we begin producing ledger-sized editions (14 inches by 17 inches) with two stories and two or more photos.

First Edition: The School Safety Patrol

When I suggested this activity to my group at the beginning of the school year, the kids had just begun using our class digital camera and were pretty excited about the idea of creating a school newspaper. For one thing, they liked having specific photographic jobs and real reasons to take photos. The writing part seemed safe enough to them since we'd be doing it together.

We made several lists of topics of interest as we decided on the focus of our first issue. The school safety patrol was an overwhelming choice to write about for our first edition. First graders were just learning about the very real jobs held by safety patrol members and how they needed to listen to these students carefully and follow their instructions. Just that very week there had been two announcements from our principal, Mario Penman, to remind children to heed warnings from the safety patrol about not running near the cafeteria and about crossing the street safely.

Photographer Assignments

After the topic of our first issue was decided, two children volunteered to meet me in the lunchroom at breakfast time the following morning. They would take pictures of students and families in the crosswalk near the front of school. Eliana's partner was late the next day, but she chose to come with me to the safety patrol areas in front of school and take charge of the photo shoot.

First, Eliana took a photo of Laura, a safety patrol member working in the upper-grade hallway. Laura explained that her job was to slow down kids who might be running in the halls. She also reminded them not to enter their classrooms until the bell rang.

Then we went outside, checking out both corners and crosswalks in front of school. After thinking things over and taking a good look, Eliana took one photo of the safety patrol stopping cars at the stop sign above the school. We then moved down the block, closer to where the action was. Eliana took three or four photos of the safety patrol members, clad in yellow helmets, red jackets, and gold reflective shoulder bands, stopping cars and safely leading families across the busy street in front of school.

Eliana was impressed with the importance of the safety patrol's job. She was impressed with her photography job, too. "It's great I got to do that and take the pictures," she said. "It was easy to do."

Recapping the Photo Shoot

Back in the classroom, Eliana explained her experiences to her classmates. She talked about her photographs, explaining why she took each one and why she had made her specific choices. Then she previewed her photos with me and chose her favorite one to be printed. When printing was completed on the printing dock (and enlarged by me on the copy machine at recess), we all looked the photograph over on our class meeting rug. It became a source to stimulate discussion and help children articulate what they already knew about the safety patrol topic. As we studied the photograph, children contributed other information to our reservoir of knowledge about the safety patrol. I quickly wrote down everything they said and read it back to them.

Since my class decided we needed to know a little more, I invited some safety patrol members to class for interviews. My students asked questions, and safety patrol members explained their jobs. Because the skill of asking good questions is especially difficult for English language learners we practiced together ahead of time. This was an especially important session for my ELLs, although all first graders need work with this skill.

As a side benefit to this whole avenue of study, my class learned the importance

Room 7 School Newspaper
October 6, 2006
Safety Patrol

Martin School Safety Patrol gets ready for duty. Luis, Salvador and Jesús wear special clothes: helmets, red jackets, and belts you can see in the dark!

Cross the street with crossing guards!

Top photo by Ms. Barrett Dragan   Bottom photo by Luis Hernandez

Figure 6–2. Our follow-up issue on the safety patrol.

of heeding safety patrol members' instructions and directions, including the previously ignored reminder to stop running near the cafeteria. We created a follow-up edition of the newspaper later in the year by taking a trip to the safety patrol room to find out how safety patrol members get ready for duty. (See Figure 6–2.)

Creating a Newspaper Empowers Kids and Gives Them Real Jobs

When children come up with a topic (with a few suggestions from me), take photographs, and investigate and build stories, they are doing authentic work. This gives them incredible self-esteem and helps them with reading, writing, critical thinking, vocabulary development, concept development, and many other skills. They understand what goes into putting stories together in a whole new way. As I observe children, I notice that our newspaper project strengthens their personal writing as well. Individual stories are much more thoughtful and of greater length. There seems to be less of a struggle to write and to understand what it takes to put words on paper. Children also *notice* more about our school and our environment and ask more questions. Being on the alert for new stories to ponder and write about enlarges their world.

Part of the impetus for this newspaper project has been our class digital camera and printer dock. Later in the year, we add another small photo printer and two more cameras. We take photos each week as we investigate stories and print pictures right in the classroom. I enlarge snapshots on the school copy machine, and we peruse them to hone ideas and work on concepts and vocabulary. We inventory what we know about the topic and talk about what we need to know to make things clear. Sometimes we go places to find things out. Other times we invite students or school personnel to come to the classroom to be interviewed.

Each Monday, we gather at our meeting place on the rug and decide on our news focus for the week. We discuss what we know and how we could go about getting information we need. Sometimes we investigate as a class; often a child will come up with a good question, and I will make a telephone call or help my reporter do so to get the needed information. If I feel a child can make a clear request for information, I make the phone call, introduce the student, and our reporter takes over, asking the question and reporting the answer to our class. (I get permission from a willing teacher before the phone call, and we set a time when a brief telephone call would not be too disruptive.) Later in the school year I sometimes send a news team of reporters and photographers to investigate a story or conduct an interview. I send only extremely reliable children on this type of assignment, and they go to a designated place, prearranged by me, such as the office or a specific teacher's classroom.

Much of what we write about, especially at the beginning of the school year, is a result of direct experience: going to an assembly, watching maintenance men fix the rain gutters after a storm, and participating in a mock search and rescue put on by our local fire department.

We don't always have a good story idea on Monday. If not, we keep eyes and ears open. I suggest to my students that they ask kids on the playground whether they are doing anything special that would make a good newspaper article.

We try to have a story in reserve for slow news weeks, such as an undated interview with someone around school—a teacher, staff member, administrator, or other person in charge of a special program, such as speech, literacy lab, or our school library.

We meet as a newspaper reporter group again each Thursday in a prewriting session. At this time the whole class of reporters discuss all they know about our topic and decide whether there is any other information they need. I jot everything down quickly in a small notebook, so I can bombard the group with results of their questions and investigations. This brainstorming session provides children with descriptive words and new vocabulary and concepts. It revs everybody up to begin writing our group story. During this time, I can clarify any terms or concepts that may not be understood. And we can find out any missing information from the office or specific students or classes.

I read notes I've taken back to the students, and they decide on that all-important title and topic sentence together. "What's the big thing you want to say?" I ask, if help is needed. The title, or headline, is the last thing we work on, since our ideas often change as we write.

And the Writing Begins

I jot down the kids' tentative headline and lead, or beginning sentence, on the giant tablet on the easel, and they help me spell the words. They listen for sounds they know and spell word-wall words (high-frequency words posted on a nearby bulletin board). I am the kids' tool for getting their words and thoughts down quickly on paper. I also supply possible beginning text or connections if students are floundering. We reread our story frequently, amending and correcting as we go along. My first graders let me know if what I write down— with their help—is what they want to say. I frequently point out how messy our draft is because we're still thinking and correcting. Later on we compare our draft with the finished product.

The first time I did this activity, children wrote interactively with me, sharing the pen. This took so much time that I don't feel we would have gotten beyond the first edition had we not modified our way of working. Shared writing—where the kids talk and spell, I write, and we all reread and revise—is the perfect way for us to get these stories put together.

Who, What, When, Where, How, and Why

We focus on making sure we tell *who* and *what* in our stories. If there is room and it seems important to the story, we add other information: *when, where, how,* and *why*. Recently Aryanna mentioned critically that we hadn't told *when* an event was held. The group decided there wasn't room to include this information, and it was not important to the story.

Developing Concepts and Getting to the Heart of a Story

A field trip to Lawrence Hall of Science in Berkeley, California, was the focus of a late-in-the-year newspaper edition. Because children were now used to putting stories together and could easily use the journalistic prompts *who, what, when, where, how,* and *why* to put our stories together, I was now focusing on vocabulary and concept development as we wrote. As we looked at our map of the area, viewed before as well as after the trip, I asked students in what direction we had traveled. After much discussion, they were able to discern that we had traveled north into San Francisco and then east across the San Francisco–Oakland Bay Bridge. The kids knew they had crossed over water but were unsure of what kind of body of water it was. Most were convinced that the bridge spanned the ocean; some thought it took us over a lake or river. It was the perfect opportunity to talk briefly about San Francisco Bay as well as some surrounding cities we had passed through, particularly San Francisco, Oakland, and Berkeley. Later in the day we made our own maps.

I continued in this way, attempting to sharpen our knowledge and vocabulary before we began to write.

Vocabulary Development: Trying Out Ways to Say Things

The show at Lawrence Hall of Science was called "Science Under the Big Top," and it featured many activities to get across concepts of physics, particularly movement and balance. I shared transparencies of two or three of the trip photos on an overhead projector to stimulate discussion and comments. The visuals helped children express themselves and get clarity on vocabulary and concepts as needed.

As we went back and read what we had written together to see if it made sense, I said things like, "There are many ways you could say this. What are some other ways?" I wrote down students' ideas on our draft, inserting each addition with a caret mark. "Which way do you want to say this?" I asked. The group was torn as they worked to choose a headline: Kids suggested "Science Field Trip"; "Circus, Circus"; and "Circus Science." The group liked "Science Field Trip" (first graders are very literal), but when Eliana told them "Circus Science" was more interesting, they voted for that headline. Most of the time we pick the headline after the story is written because it makes more sense then.

One part of the story that took a little time was deciding what to call the people who work in a circus. The group thought *circus actors* would be a good title, but Hector mentioned that people in shows *perform*. It was a quick leap to introduce (or wait for someone to think of) the term *performer*. *Tightrope* was another term the children were not familiar with. When I introduced it, I asked them to guess what people were called who walked across the tightrope. They liked the term *tightrope walkers* and also *high-wire walkers*. They decided that tightrope walkers had to balance when they walked the tightrope. This led to other modifications of the story and use of the words *tightrope walker* and *balance*.

I don't want to take over the authorship of the children's stories. I try to introduce vocabulary and concepts I feel will expand and enlighten without intruding on the children's words or thought processes. I want this newspaper writing session to be an exciting interlude and one that is based on my students' experiences and their need to know. I try to create an environment that encourages kids' interest in their news, and I want them to feel the story is *theirs*. I also hope they will be able to read it, understand it, and enjoy it when they get their copies of their newspaper.

Going to Press

After my students have helped me write their thoughts down on large chart paper, and we have reread and revised our thoughts, I type the story. One or two children help me with the layout by using tape rolls to attach photos to the letter-sized computer paper with the story printed on it. Then it's time we go to press: The children and I quietly sneak into the faculty room, which now sports a great new copy machine. The kids sit on the sofas (with books they have brought to occupy them) while I push buttons and get ready to run our page. They are now able to tell me which buttons to push, and many could probably set up the machine themselves if they could reach the controls. The machine is new. I don't push my luck. I push the buttons and set up the machine.

Then comes a moment of great fizz and excitement as the first copy prints and rolls out. Since the paper is 14 inches by 17 inches, and the story and photos are enlarged (approximately 110 to 140 percent, depending on the page), we are able to see well enough to proofread our paper together, right there by the copy machine. Invariably, when we skip this step, there is a typo (made by me) or some kind of other mistake. We all learn the hard way to read things over before we go to press. I now print about five sample copies for the children to peruse in proofreading groups they organize themselves. The first time I included this step, Ed Fristoe, our school psychologist, came into the faculty room, and we had a couple of moments to chat. A child came running up to me, paper in hand, to point out an error. I was so proud of her. Ed almost passed out from pure surprise. It's amazing what kids can accomplish when they get the chance!

When they proofread one issue, several children found that we had placed two photos on the page with two stories, but the pictures and stories didn't match. When we repositioned the photos, it all made sense. This careful proofreading saved a lot of paper, time, and embarrassment!

When the newspaper is proofed to everyone's satisfaction, we print 14-by-17-inch copies: one for each classroom, one for the office, and a few extras. We put a copy in each teacher's mailbox. We also print two newspapers for each of my first graders—one to take home immediately, and one to keep in a collection at school.

Each child has a newspaper binder with many plastic page protectors filled with folded copies of our ledger-sized paper. I fold the newspapers in half for the kids, but they each slide their copies into the page protectors and then put them into their binders, with the newest edition on top. Children have discovered that when they turn their binder horizontally and lift up the cover, they see the top half of the newspaper page. When they lift their page protector up to turn the page, they see the bottom half. In this way they have large-print editions they can read. We frequently read these as a group, enjoying yet again our memories of highlights of the year.

I will give these inexpensive plastic binders and their contents to the children at the end of the year. In the meantime, since I no longer want to send binders home each week and risk them getting lost—as happened in November—the children can take their additional newspaper home on publication day. This step is important, because Friday, when the newspaper is indeed hot off the press, is the day my kids want to look at it and read it over and over again. And their families look forward to getting their new editions.

Angelina recapped the whole newspaper experience with a short story and drawings. (See Figure 6–3.)

Newspaper Big Book

I found an old big book, not a popular one in my class, and I paper clipped large blank pieces of construction paper to each page, as well as to the cover. On top of each white page, I paper clipped one newspaper issue. In this way we may also enjoy our school press as a big book. Sometimes we read it together; the children also enjoy reading it themselves with friends. Even though they have their own binders, they like seeing the whole page at a glance, in book form.

Delivery Service

The trip to the office to deliver our paper is part of our celebration of the whole week's news team work. When other children or members of our school commu-

Figure 6–3. Angelina writes about the newspaper experience.

nity are featured in our newspaper, we deliver issues to those people too. Then we go back to our classroom to read our own copies, comment on the paper, and do an essential wrap-up. These times are brief, with very little criticism. Most of the time, we are pretty excited and jazzed up about what we have accomplished. The kids love to try to read their newspapers again and again. Literacy takes a great jump through this project. And the children feel such pride in accomplishment.

Litzi looked back and marveled at her personal success midway through the year when she said, "My mom *knows* I'm a reporter and a photographer 'cause I got to take the pictures at Back-to-School Night." And Dariana gave our project high praise one Friday when we returned from our newspaper delivery route. "I think we're really authors," she said with a great big sigh of satisfaction.

Enlisting Staff Ideas for Relevant Stories

At a faculty meeting early in the school year I explained our newspaper project briefly and requested faculty input for story ideas. Since that time, my newspaper staff of first graders has worked on several stories involving students in other classes. One newspaper issue featured Juan Carlos, a fourth grader who helps younger children pick books in our school library.

I was very impressed when I overheard Juan Carlos explaining a book on Diego Rivera, the Mexican painter and muralist, to two of my first graders. He was telling them that in the book he had learned a lot about how Mayan Indians had lived and how they made their homes and their clothing. I don't think my kids understood all of this, but they were interested, since a big kid was paying attention to them.

As a result, one of our class members photographed Juan Carlos reading to these two students, and the group requested that he come down to our room and be interviewed about his work in the library. Ultimately, Juan Carlos became the focus of our next edition.

After a recent assembly about the creation of musical instruments from found objects, Eileen Christopherson's kindergarten class created paper-bag-and-junk rhythm instruments and formed their own band. At a faculty meeting Eileen clued me in to what her children were doing. My students were interested and decided this was a great topic for a story. Within two weeks our newspaper featured the Room 2 Calabasa Band playing their homemade rhythm instruments. My class visited the band at practice time in their classroom. They asked questions about how the instruments were made. These activities helped my children feel they knew enough to write the story.

Of course, kindergartners were each given a special newspaper page to "read" and take home.

Freedom of the Press

Working on our newspaper project gives our class a small amount of freedom to check out stories, pursue leads, poke around, and try out ideas. Sometimes we stay at assemblies after other classes have left and use this time for any questions we may have for future newspaper stories. After all, we're investigative reporters. We have to follow where our curiosity leads us, do some decision making together, and put out the best newspaper we are capable of creating. And we have to do a lot of critical thinking and analyzing along the way.

This project, and others in this book, is a prime example of Lev Vygotsky's theory of the zone of proximal development. In his book *Thought and Language* (1986), the Russian psychologist theorizes that students can achieve much more when "scaffolded," or supported by adult help at the reaching edge of their growth, than they could accomplish on their own. With our newspaper project I feel I have done my best scaffolding, and I have seen incredible results in just one school year.

Here are some newspaper stories children have written in just one school year with my help in getting them going and making leaps when they were stuck (I found that my assistance became more sophisticated as the year went on):

- "Safety Patrol"
- "Back-to-School Night"
- "Our Librarian"
- "Help at the Library" (featuring Juan Carlos, a student library aide)
- "The Firefighters"
- "Happy Halloween!"
- "Famous Author Visits" (Stephen Cary came to class to work on an ESL project for the revised edition of his book *Working with Second Language Learners: Answers to Teachers' Top Ten Questions.*)
- "Aryanna Wins Contest"
- "Our Custodian"
- "Happy Thanksgiving!" (how Martin School students celebrated Thanksgiving at school)
- "Our Letter from Antarctica" (Paul Nicklen, National Geographic photographer, wrote a personal letter to our class.)
- "School Board Visits" (School board members came to see our newspaper project and ended up being interviewed for a story.)
- "The Polar Express" (first grade's winter storytelling event)
- "Our Winter Program"
- "Rainy Day Problem" (Maintenance department fixed the roof.)
- "Kindergarten Rock Star Band"
- "Speech Class"
- "The Penguin Lady" (visit from Marsha Oviatt, Antarctica traveler)
- "Reading Is Fun!"
- "Jump Rope for Heart!"
- "Spotlight Students"
- "The Limo Ride"
- "Wild Things" (Six wild animals visited school.)
- "100's Day"
- "News Team Visits Office" (This included interviews with our principal, Mario Penman; our secretary, Colleen Morello; and our office clerk, Rosalinda Flores.)
- "School Talent Show"
- "Newspaper Know-How" (steps we go through to produce the paper each week)
- "Awards Assembly"
- "Youth Art Show"

- "Circus Science" (science field trip)
- "Caring for the Flag" (night custodian's job of taking down the flags each day)
- "Magical Moonshine Theater"
- "The Xylophone Show"
- "Easter Egg Hunt"
- "City Hall Trip"
- "Our Caterpillars Change"
- "Our Inventor!" (Edward's invention of a patterned cube)
- "Happy Mother's Day!"
- "Book Fair"
- "Ballet Folklórico"
- "Vocabulary Parade"
- "Our Balloon Man"
- "Marlo Rides the Bus" (Marlo won a county contest, and his photo and art are featured on a SamTrans bus in San Mateo County, California.)

Writing and publishing a newspaper gives kids inside knowledge of how newspapers work and their importance to a community. It also gives students more intense interest in reading, not just their own paper but other newspapers as well, such as their *Scholastic News* or *Weekly Reader* issues and our social studies newspaper-format lessons. Magazine reading has increased since we began this project. Many children now choose a magazine as well as a book when we go to the school library.

7

Taking to the Streets

A good life is a learning life.
—Lucy Sprague Mitchell, Bank Street College

A natural extension of our photojournalism experience is to take to the streets and neighborhoods near school, find out about local businesses, and see where our curiosity leads us. As Lucy Sprague Mitchell, Bank Street founder, writes in her classic book *Our Children and Our Schools*, "We need to build a curriculum that enables children to grow in power to think, to observe, to express themselves, to live with others, and to care about others outside their own narrow personal group" (1951, 353). Active learning suits the bill!

I believe that taking children on excursions and engaging them in authentic learning experiences stimulates them to learn in all subject areas. As Mitchell says, this approach helps children grow as thinkers, scientists, and artists. And I believe it honors their natural curiosity and propensity to investigate everything in their world. It opens up the world to them.

Checking Out What's Going on at School

Although we take one or two full-day bus field trips each year as a first-grade group, approximately every two weeks, usually for half an hour to an hour or so in the morning or afternoon, I also take my class on small investigative journeys. Sometimes the trip is near and quite brief: as close as the cafeteria, where we see food being delivered before lunch. We see Usha, the cafeteria lady, heating and serving the food that was delivered; Roy, the custodian, sweeping and performing all kinds of thoughtful jobs for us; the tanbark company delivering a truckload of material to the play equipment area; district workers fixing the roof; and so on.

When the kids talked to the men fixing our roof and drainpipe after a storm last winter, it became one of their favorite newspaper stories. Later that spring they checked out the painters who were sprucing up our school with fresh new color and trim. My first graders look at everything with eyes wide open—they always want to know what's going on.

The Neighborhood

Other times we leave the school grounds for the neighborhood to see what we can find out by visiting one of the local businesses. Martin Elementary is in the older part of South San Francisco, near several historic homes and buildings in the downtown area. When I walk to town with my first graders, we get a chance to notice unusual buildings with old-fashioned trim, staircases, doorways, rounded rooms, and unusual rooflines. We share the cameras to take photos. Children love to sketch and photograph City Hall, the old courthouse, and the old Carnegie Library on Grand Avenue. There are a variety of stores selling Mexican cookies and pastries, Chinese food, musical equipment, and other goods and services. The old post office features a mural painted fifty years ago, and fruits and vegetables in front of the outdoor market near school are polished and brilliantly colored. There are many interesting things to see. Once their eyes get in tune, children notice lots of details, textures, colors, and shapes.

I always scope it all out ahead of time, making appointments when necessary. I know some of the learning possibilities, but I try to keep some of them under my hat so children can make some discoveries of their own. Before our trip we discuss things children are curious about and want to know. We practice asking questions. This helps not only English learners but the rest of our class as well. First graders characteristically have difficulty asking questions and want to tell you their own experiences instead.

When we go out and about, we bring two or three digital cameras so that a few children at a time can photograph details of interest to them. I just pass cameras around, always making sure the students getting them are paying attention and have the camera straps looped around their wrists. This has prevented many a dropped camera. Other children may be busy sketching or taking notes in their small folded-paper booklets or talking with friends. Some are much more involved in picture taking than others.

I shoot a lot of photos of children taking pictures. I love the expressions on their faces, their posture, and the ways they look at things as they decide what to snap. It's always a surprise to see what the kids do photograph. Once in a while one of them turns the knob to video by mistake, and I really get an eyeful. Until I checked on the photos taken during a recent trip, I had no idea that a few furtive souls were sliding down the banister outside City Hall as I was speaking with another child.

Our City Hall trip was my favorite excursion last year. We had a real reason to go: children in our class had their work on display as part of a citywide youth art show. We also wanted to see some of the historic buildings in town and check out the Mexican Market.

Eavesdropping—A Great Way to Learn

I watch and listen. Eavesdropping is a great way to find out what is going on with children. I learn a lot on these jaunts, and so do they. When we headed into San Francisco and Berkeley on a recent bus trip, I could hear all manner of fascinating comments: "Ohhh! Look at the towers!" "The city is sooo big." "The bridge is crossing the water and there's like an island." "Guys are building stuff over there!" (The children were referring to the crews working on the new span of the San Francisco–Oakland Bay Bridge.)

The ten-minute walk into downtown South San Francisco inspired children just as much as an all-day trip and taught me a lot about the kids too. Sagar is fascinated with cars of all types, and as we walked to downtown South San Francisco, he kept up a running commentary. He knows a lot more than I do about this subject. Several children wanted to take pictures of City Hall as the clock tower appeared in the distance. I can't believe how excited they were to see this piece of architecture. Living so close to the main street of town, they had seen this building many times. But when we are photographing or sketching, we all see things in a whole new way.

The kids commented on everything: every flower and bush, many of the houses, pets in the yard, people they know, good places to play. When we got to town they couldn't wait to get to the outside steps of City Hall and pose for a picture. And they all gasped when we entered the building and saw the black panels with student art displayed. The children spent a few minutes looking at the art and posing for pictures with friends in front of their artwork, but the main draw was the giant velvet-covered stairway under a large chandelier. There were tantalizing views of an upstairs floor with wooden railings all around. One child sat there alone at the bottom, looking up, for quite a while before others discovered the view. My kids all clustered on the staircase, in awe, some just looking and others sketching or jotting down things they wanted to remember. Later on when I looked at their mini sketchbooks, I saw that several had drawn the chandelier above and the railings and curious spaces upstairs.

The assistant to the city manager came out to speak with us, pausing at the upstairs railing. (Could it be that she heard us?) My kids went into interview mode. They asked questions and wrote down comments of interest. I found out that this was someone I knew, Susan Kennedy, a former firefighter who used to organize our school fire prevention programs. She gave us quite a bit of her time. Children were impressed, and we were invited back to take a tour.

The kids wanted to know everything: who were those people whose pictures were on the wall (present and former mayors), just what *was* in the rooms upstairs, and so on. I decided we would take that tour before school was over.

Outside the building I counted and saw that I still had the full crew of students, both cameras, and all three mothers. We headed for the Latin American bakery on the next block, checking out things and reading signs in store windows on the way. I divided kids into little groups, and we brainstormed some ideas of things we wanted to notice in the store. Mexican pastries were a great item of fascination on our little tour, but the pigs' feet won the prize for most interesting thing in the market—until we got to the ice-cream counter. As we were voting on whether I would purchase cookies or ice cream for the group, the store owner introduced himself. He became the children's hero by offering them each a free ice cream. Kids marveled over this all the way back to school. Before selecting their ice-cream bars, two student reporters snapped photos, and a few children asked relevant questions about the cash registers and the people who worked in the store. Litzi ran into her father, who was shopping and hadn't realized she would be there.

When we scrubbed up from the ice creams upon our return to school, kids couldn't stop talking about the trip. Since spring break was starting the next day, it was now or never to give them time to express their thoughts and impressions. After a brief interlude, we found ourselves printing off two photos and creating our second newspaper edition of the day. The headline of the second edition read "City Hall Trip" and featured a photo of Susan Kennedy, the assistant to the city manager, being interviewed by Luis, as he wrote in his small notebook. The second story talked about the visit to Mercado Panadería Hernández. It showed a good view of the store facade and three children eating ice cream.

Children took the newspaper home to read and talk about, and parents got a firsthand look at what we'd been up to at school that day.

I really like these little trips much better than our somewhat unwieldy field trips with seventy first graders. I think small jaunts are more personal. We can talk with each other and share the experiences more easily, and it's certainly easier to sketch, make notes, and pass around cameras. When I asked the children which kind of trip they preferred, the results were divided. I think the trip with the free ice creams won out.

We have also taken small trips to La Tapatilla, a tortilla factory nearby, the Grand Avenue Library, and the post office, where we mailed letters and took a brief tour. Publishing a newspaper about these excursions makes them seem even more important, and our learning takes on a whole new meaning. It's real.

With the digital camera it's easy to delete unwanted shots later. Digitals give us a lot more freedom in our picture taking. We can take risks, try new things, and we don't worry about wasting camera shots.

The digital camera and the printer dock are really convenient for obtaining almost immediate pictures. We can preview photos first, just as soon as we get back to the classroom, and only print a few we especially like. This cuts down on expenses for ink cartridges and paper.

Using Copies of Photos on the Overhead Projector

Photocopies of excursion pictures are great takeoff points for discussion, especially if I make acetate transparencies so that we may look at the enlarged photos on a screen or the classroom wall. I recently discovered an inexpensive item called a card reader. I download photos to the card reader and plug it into the computer. This is an easy way to view our images and even have a slide show!

Often I print copies of a representative snapshot or two on the large copier in the faculty room. I place the photo on a template with an area for the picture and lines underneath. I make a class set of copies. Children can write below the image and add further illustrations with pen if they wish. This works especially well when we have focused on the enlarged image and talked about it. These papers form a great record of students' learning as well as a nice memory of the minitrip. When we surround ourselves with new ideas, creativity flourishes. We learn a great deal collaboratively.

When we return from the trip, we don't necessarily talk about it right away. Waiting a day or so gives children a chance to process information and digest their experiences. These investigative journeys enable children to grow in their power to think, to observe, and to express themselves. They learn about what it means to live with others, what we need to survive. They learn to care about people outside their own families and personal groups.

Then and Now

South San Francisco is an old city by West Coast standards; one hundred years old in 2008. When I take my first graders to town, we can step back in time just a bit and see some remnants of days long ago. This is especially true on Grand Avenue, the main street. We have an old photo, taken a century ago, that shows horses and buggies on a wide dirt road. People are dressed in clothing typical of the times, and there is not a car to be seen. The main street we see today gives children a focus for their cameras and also helps make the concept of time passage more believable. (See Chapter 5.)

Kids have great eyes for detail. This comes out in the writing they do about their photos and in the stories they tell. We build a model of the town on the rug, creating buildings and street scenes from cut construction paper taped to paper rolls so they stand upright. Children enter the scene as well, adding cutout photos of themselves and their families. It is like a giant theatre, with our own movable true-to-life cutouts. (See "Box Theater Art" in Chapter 4.)

We can use photocopies of pictures of the city to create whole new two-dimensional collage scenes, adding in photos of ourselves.

Trips to town lend themselves to wonderful art projects, including collages that intermix photographs with drawings, Styrofoam prints of interesting old build-ings, and large tempera paintings of local architecture and scenes. The children and I make a collage of photographs together. The children write about it or their own special photographs if they choose. Going to town helps re-create the past and make it more believable to young students. We explore the neighborhood and learn all we can about how it functions, the people who live there, and goods and services available, now and in the past. We learn what it means to be a commu-nity. The cameras help us to see and understand.

Some minitrip (and photo) opportunities within just a few blocks of school include:

- candy factory
- meat market
- park
- U.S. post office
- grocery stores
- several types of bakeries
- car wash
- service stations
- tortilla factory
- city library
- historical society room in local library
- City Hall
- old courthouse
- fire station
- police station
- outdoor fruit and vegetable market
- restaurants and cafes
- florist shop
- hardware store
- dry cleaners
- bread factory
- music store

8

Imagination Stations
Giving Students Opportunities to Investigate and Learn Their Way

You mean I can really cut it and write in it and put pictures in it?
And we can do pasting things in it and whatever we want, like crumble it?
—Alejandro, first grader

My first graders were incredulous when I gave them each a well-used children's magazine to cut, paste, write in, and "recycle their way." After listening to me talk all year about taking care of books, how to turn pages, being careful not to write in books, and so on, now they found me encouraging them to write, paint, draw, cut, paste, bend, fold, pop up, and crunch the pages of their magazines.

"It's like recycling," I told them. "Make something different and wild and interesting and turn an old magazine into an exciting adventure. You could cut out parts of some pages; you could add things in, like photographs, words, your own stories and drawings, cut and torn paper, or other magazine pictures. See how you can make it all connect in ways that are fun to look at and read."

These ideas sounded good to my kids, and they dove right in.

This altered-magazine project is one of several *imagination stations*, or learning centers, I have developed to give my students time to work on things that matter to them. The altered-magazine craft is a takeoff on a project called *altered books* that is often seen in book making exhibitions and craft shows. I prefer using the magazines for my project because I am afraid if I use old books there might be a crazy carryover in book treatment. Magazines seem one step removed. We'll still treat books as carefully as we can. And besides, it's obvious from looking that these magazines are not in brand-new condition. I put aside worn children's magazines for this project and ask my friendly city librarian to save some for me as well. It's nice to have a large selection so that children can choose the one they want.

Although students may later work on altered magazines in small-group centers, I prefer to introduce the activity with the whole group to teach everyone to manage it. I give out magazines as if they were empty sketchbooks for my students to use for their creative work. But the magazines, unlike blank booklets, already have some bits they can use: colored photos, textures, advertising, drawings, words, stories, and articles. The magazines provide a starting place for collage, and a place to put things. They are the base and background for creativity. Kids just use what's there and change it in interesting ways. This project gives them a real taste of freedom and a place to play and write and visualize on paper.

Altered Postcards

A variation of the previous project is to use old postcards or greeting cards instead of magazines. This is a good lead-in to the project and gives children a small, focused experience of using old or found objects to create new personal artwork, writing, and photographic collage. Empty cereal boxes are another alternative. Kids can use photographs and mixed media to invent themselves on the Wheaties or Cheerios box just as if they've won the Olympics or achieved another goal important to them!

A Place for Bits and Pieces

To facilitate smooth management of our imagination stations, I provide each student with a project box to keep things in or ask children to bring one from home. It is crucial that each child has a special place for all the scraps and treasures that may be used as the projects evolve.

Last year our custodian cleaned out a storeroom and left the perfect boxes up for grabs in the faculty room. These were kept in children's cubbies under their backpacks. A large plastic bag could also be used for each student's collection of paper scraps, photo bits, glue sticks, magazines, stickers, stars, and partially thought out creations. My editor, Jim Strickland, reminded me that unused pizza boxes are also good choices for kids to keep things in, as are shoe boxes. Teachers are very adept at asking the business community for materials and supplies like this. If all else fails, gallon-sized freezer-weight plastic bags will also work.

Generic Supplies for Each Table

As we learn some ideas for working on the altered-magazine project, I provide a shoe box or cardboard soft drink tray with supplies for each table: marking pens, crayons, construction paper crayons, colored pencils, paper punches, rubber stamps and stamp pads, and so on. Each child is also given a sampling of photocopied pictures taken of classmates. Kids love to use these images of friends in their work.

Children know where scissors, extra glue sticks, paper, and paper scraps are kept in the classroom. They are free to use what they need, but they know that everything must be put back and cleaned up if they want to have this type of creative art and writing interlude again!

Here is a list of supplies that are great for this project:

- photographs and photocopies of pictures
- old calendars and magazines; cereal boxes
- postcards, greeting cards
- a variety of stationery and kinds of writing papers, lined and unlined
- buttons
- metal washers
- stars, stickers, ribbon, string
- small flat toys
- wallpaper sample books
- sticky-backed geometric shapes
- sequins
- glitter pens
- marking pens
- tissue paper

Literature Leads the Way

As a way into the altered-magazine lesson, I shared David Wiesner's Caldecott Award–winning book *The Three Pigs* (2001) with my class. In this visual treat, the wolf and the three pigs totally exit the page and leave the traditional story. Pieces of other stories and folk and fairy tales appear on the scene with their characters, and some parts of stories are never quite the same again. This is the mind-set I was looking for to introduce this transforming magazine project. Another book that is a great imagination starter is *The Flying Dragon Room,* by Audrey Wood (2000). A boy named Patrick uses some magical tools to create his own busy world, interconnected by a "Ziggety-Zaggity Ladder" and other magical means. The book teems with creatures large and small. It includes a bubble room, a screaming chamber, a gravity-defying room, a pirate ship, and even a wild animal room. Details are unique and may offer suggestions to students as they work to come up with their own creations.

Another picture book that fuels creative thought is *Flotsam*, a wordless book by David Wiesner (2006). In this Caldecott Award winner, a boy finds an old-fashioned camera at the beach. When he has the film developed he finds astonishing photos of an underwater world: a wind-up fish, an octopus in an armchair holding story hour, and portraits of children around the world and through the ages. The book leaves the readers space for their own imagined worlds and propels kids to invent them.

When children work in their magazines, they are really doing collage: making pictures by gluing pieces of cloth, paper, photographs, and magazine cutouts to the magazine background. They can add crayon and pen drawings and pieces of writing. If they wish, there can be a specific theme, such as things that are important to them, outer space adventures, a trip to the rain forest, and so on. As I have found with my first graders and also the intermediate-level after-school enrichment group, it can take more than one session before children feel comfortable with collage. But throughout each work period they are totally absorbed and seem to be problem solving their own personal pieces of artwork. This is a great project to develop critical thinking. It is important that students have time to share and talk about their work after each session.

All it takes is one child making a breakthrough to set the class afire with ideas. When Eliana cut a magazine page "frame" for the photo I had taken of her with her father, everyone in my class raced to do something similar. Luis' idea of putting his cutout photograph in the crook of an elephant's trunk excited a lot of kids. And when Dariana's magazine page showed her photo peeking out from behind a rainbow, the rest of my group started loosening up and having fun with magazines, art, and the written word. Just about anything goes. There's no wrong way to do this project. I want kids to have the opportunities to find their own ways with the materials and develop their own unique ideas. (See Figure 8–1.)

Here are a few sample ideas to get kids started on altered magazines or postcards. They can

- cut out letters of their names or special words and glue them on the cover of the magazine or in a place of their choice
- write two or three sentences to go with a photograph they like and place them somewhere in the magazine
- cut out a few "windows" or "doors" in magazine pages and put something behind them, on the next page
- use one magazine page as the background for a collage of personal things that are special
- make flaps that lift up to show special images underneath
- make a special photo or drawing pop-up
- add on interesting scraps and bits of paper, beads, stickers, yarn, magazine cutouts, and other items that relate to the page in progress

Another lesson that will help free kids up to create is to show them some ways to fold and pleat paper, how to make a simple pop-up, or how to make flaps that lift up to show something interesting underneath. A great reference book for some simple and involved pop-up ideas is *How to Make Pop-Ups*, by Joan Irvine (1988). She is a pop-up genius and is known in Canada as the Pop-Up Lady.

Making Mini-Books, by Sherri Haab (2002), is another wonderful reference. Once children understand these paper sculpture techniques, they can use them in a myriad of ways to express themselves creatively as they invent, craft, and construct using a magazine or piece of environmental print.

Figure 8–1. Eliana's altered magazine.

Imagination stations are my approach for giving students some freedom to learn and to process their learning independently. A variation on teacher-planned learning centers, they emphasize the children's control and decision making as they work on specific topics. These stations are periods where students can think, work, play, listen to each other, create, innovate, and teach themselves. I like to set up these stations thematically, providing some ideas and materials and a suggested focus, and then give children the most helpful tool for success: time. I try to keep my influence to a minimum and give children a chance to make discoveries. I want them to make some choices about what they want to learn and have time to try things out and to process their learning. An important part of each session is the period for sharing afterward. This special wrap-up time can result in an explosion of ideas.

Children learn a great deal at these centers and have a lot of fun as well. As poet and author Diane Ackerman says in her book *Deep Play* (2000), "Play is our brain's favorite way of learning."

When I use imagination stations to pursue the theme of photography, I set up the following areas with suggestions and materials children can use. My students are also free to express and follow their ideas about ways to use stations. Sometimes the whole class will be interested in working on one activity at the same time. This large-group time is important for introducing an idea and a station. Other times the kids prefer to work in small groups. Following are stations I have used for our photography projects.

Altered Magazines and Postcards

Materials: Magazines, postcards, greeting cards (cut off backs of greeting cards to create postcards), paper scraps, old calendars

Art supplies: glue sticks, construction paper, wallpaper scraps, photocopies of children's photos, scissors, watercolor pencils, marking pens, construction paper crayons, and so on

Writing About Photographs

Materials: Children's own photos and photocopies of photos; a variety of writing papers and writing implements: pencils, pens, and fine-line marking pens; tape; large freezer bags (helpful for keeping personal materials in one place)

The freezer bag is kept in each student's project box. Completed work can be kept in memory book binders (see next section). The students are very motivated to write about these photographs. As Robert Coles says in his book *Their Eyes Meeting the World: The Drawings and Paintings of Children*, pictures offer "all kinds of chances: a chance to demonstrate artistic skill, aesthetic capacity, imaginative resourcefulness; a chance to make a personal statement, to say something that matters to one's heart and mind and soul; a chance to indicate what one knows" (1992, 6). I believe that children's photographs offer the same opportunities. They give others a chance to see and to understand what the children see.

Some of what I've seen through the photos and writings of my students are stories about special people: a grandfather who lost his eye in a motorcycle accident; a picture of a fifth grader's father, young and skinny on his bicycle years ago (who had just gotten his second job in Mexico at the age of twelve); a little sister who almost died at birth but survived; a mom and dad who loved each other so much that they "got married" and "then the dad brought flowers." The students' story writing and oral language are heartfelt, and the beauty of this is enhanced by the sincerity and playfulness of the tellings. For me these stories are especially endearing and evocative when children have not yet mastered the language.

Photography helps children bring us their stories. As Robert Coles says, "In some of these stories live the truths of their lives" (1990).

Organizing and Sharing Memory Books or Scrapbooks
Materials: memory books (binders with plastic sleeves to hold photos and writing), variety of papers to be used as background for photos and writing, paper scraps, glue sticks or tape

Children work for most of the school year on their memory books, photo albums, or scrapbooks. Sometimes there is even feverish activity on the last day of school to finish writing and get those photos and drawings in the binders that will finally go home.

As they look through their photos, their writings, their photo books, and memories of their lives on the last day of school, some children are still writing, and others are cutting photos to create last-minute collages. I feel that children have gained some kind of *power* through their personal endeavors. They are focused deeply, looking inward, and totally in control. I glance at a child who gets it only some of the time, but when I ask him to focus on his photos and his album, he begins to write and is soon involved. Betsy is in another realm altogether, deep into writing about her feelings about her parents, underneath photos of each of them hugging her. For all the children, this stolen time on the final day of school is a last-minute scramble to connect their photos and their writing with their lives. Hopefully, when they take these treasures home they will continue working on them, but whether they do or not, they have *this* time, and now they are—almost all of them—making the most of it.

I believe that our family stories and photos can shape us. My hope is that the children's binders and collections of writing and photographs about their year of successes will help propel them onward, in confidence, toward many positive, enriching experiences in their lives ahead—and help them, in the words of Charles Dickens in *David Copperfield*, to be "the heroes of their own lives."

Photographic Storytelling: Using Photos to Generate Stories
Materials: Photography books and photos (photocopies of photos, in plastic page protectors)

During their time in school, children are sometimes cautioned to be quiet and urged not to talk. One of the things I love about this project is that it supports opposing behavior: this center will work only if children *do* talk and work together to express themselves and tell meaningful stories. Perhaps that is why kids enjoy this center so much. They can be themselves and tell things as *they* see them!

Class Books: RealePublishing (See Chapter 5 for more information.)
   Materials: Digital camera photos, computer with RealeBooks template

Note: Teacher help is needed at this station.

Magic Story Box
   Materials: Box with a variety of imaginative props: hats, glasses, scarves, gloves, aprons, costumes, wands, stars, headbands, glasses, moustaches, and so on; interesting picture books; digital camera (optional)

Kids love this story box—partly for the suspense to see what is in the box on any given day (sometimes new things magically appear there) partly because children love to pretend and to perform. Frequently they are eager to act out things they can't say in English. The group works together to develop characters and a story. Children may also take pictures and view them on the digital camera. Selected photos may be printed out later, on the computer, the printer dock, or the small photo printer. Photos then cycle to the memory book center, so children can write about them and compose their stories about the images. This is a collaborative process and helps children with language acquisition. They are so engrossed, and having so much fun, that they sometimes do not realize how hard they are working to make language comprehensible.

Vocabulary Center
   Materials: Dictionaries and books of words, student notebooks for collecting words and illustrating them

Additional stations that require adult help may replace the *RealeBook* center:

- Set up a station at the computer where the teacher is available to help children download their photographs. Or plan a teacher station at the printer dock or photo printer, so children can print their photos.
- Another station gives children opportunities to take pictures. About four or five students with a camera or two groups of five children can manage this photographic station, each group with a camera. Children can photograph each other or take photographs of things of interest to them.

All of these stations further self-confidence, language, and creativity.

9

Photo-Essays
Publishing a Literary Magazine— *an After-School Enrichment Project*

All the fun's in how you say a thing.
—Robert Frost

Faces of my after-school enrichment students light up like beacons when they get a first glimpse of their published literary magazine, *Special Days: Reflections on Things That Really Matter.* The booklet, complete with their essays, poetry, and photography, is a culmination of two months of hard work. These eight fourth and fifth graders worked after school and at home to ferret out an idea, a simple detail, an unforgettable moment that helped shape their lives—one they would want to mull over and write about. Some students wrote of seemingly ordinary everyday events—one special moment among many. Others described a definitive life-changing experience. Some of these stories are happy and reflect one of those times you never want to forget. Others are sad; all are poignant.

I wanted to explore the close connection of story and photography to help kids write photo-essays that would extend and polish their writing skills. I wanted to help them write something truly important to them. I believed that photographs would add another dimension to their thinking and their writing, and that inclusion of their own pictures would illuminate their life experiences and enrich their telling of them. I also wanted students to have the opportunity to create and publish a reflective piece of their own writing in a literary document they could be proud of.

My students used disposable cameras to take relevant photos—pictures that meant something to them. And they went through photographs they had at home as well, in the quest to find a special image to publish with their writing. There was a moment of quiet, followed by nervous laughter when students got their first quick looks at the magazine and then received their own copies. We read their work together, and they seemed satisfied and pleased. They enjoyed asking each other questions and talking about their very personal memoirs and photographs.

A Story, a Story

We began this project by telling stories to each other in our small after-school group, introducing ourselves by choosing two brief personal and meaningful incidents from our lives and then telling these short anecdotes in the third person. This technique, which immediately gets participants into storytelling mode, is one I learned in a *Word Weaving* (1983) workshop written and taught by Catherine Horne Farrell in the 1980s. Zellerbach Family Fund sponsored the project, and staff development workshops were given to educators throughout California. I used several of Farrell's ideas in my after-school program, and I also used some of the books I had shared with my first graders (see Chapter 2). The most evocative for me were *Family Pictures/Cuadros de familia* (1990) and *In My Family/En mi familia* (2000), both by Carmen Lomas Garza.

Garza says a lot with just a short paragraph on a page and an illustration done with paint or cut paper on the facing page. I wanted to make a point to my students that our goal was quality, not quantity, and that perhaps they could get to the heart of their own special memoir if they looked at their stories pointedly, in brief. One reason behind this suggestion was our shortage of time.

I gave kids disposable cameras, pencils, pens, and notebooks. We brainstormed about important memories and shared a few. Students did some quickwrites to gather their thoughts. They took cameras home and explored other ideas through the reflective lens.

Luis got the idea right away. "Focus and magnify the moment," he said, and he did, when he wrote about the awe and grandeur of the environment on his first camping trip. Martha's special moment was about playing catch with her grandfather before he died. "My grandpa liked to play catch with me so much that he was already out the door when he saw that my brother and I came to play with him. He loved our time together as much as we did."

María wrote a moving piece about how hard her parents worked to buy their first house and then how difficult it was to move away from the small home her family had shared with many family members. "I was sad to leave my aunt and uncle and cousins, but this house was better," she wrote. "We weren't 'squished' any more." María chose to use older photos to illustrate her photo-essay: pictures of her home and family before and after moving to their new home.

The camera worked as a tool to help students express themselves. Daisy's story about her little brother and a motorcycle was enhanced and illuminated by the photo of the two-year-old astride his father's Harley. And in another essay she told of her great love for her sister, Michelle, who had taken care of her when she had pink eye and the family thought she was going blind. In the photo she took, you can see her strong affection for her sister, and in the tone of her piece, you can hear her awe when she describes ways her sister tried to help her.

I loved the moment Ronaldo chose to illuminate with words and a photo: the time, after days of struggling with a class assignment, he came up with a fantasy story about a gang of penguins that ordered pizza. He included a cutout drawing of one of these penguins in a photo collage incorporating his own picture. Ronaldo wrote of his relief in getting past what he called "writer's block" and his deep-down excitement at his classmates' positive responses when he read his story aloud. "Everyone laughed and laughed," he said. "Being a writer is a good opportunity to share your ideas." The title of Ronaldo's work was "A Writer."

Alejandro took a photo of a special window and used it as an anchor for his writing. "I took a view from our kitchen window," he said. "This picture is cool because every day for breakfast, lunch, dinner, and even when I do my homework at this table, I can see the San Francisco Bay, the San Mateo Bridge, and the planes flying out and into the airport." Alejandro said he took pictures of people and things he wanted to remember now and in the future, so he "would know some things that were important to [him] when [he] was eleven."

Angelina described her best friends and said they decided to be special friends because "each one of [them] was lonely without someone to play with, and [they] all started playing with each other. [They] got used to being together."

Perhaps the most poignant story for me was Mikee Anne's narrative, "The Day We Left Manila." She described her heartbreak at leaving not only some family members and friends but also her dad. Mikee Anne's photo was taken just before she left for the United States—a picture of her in an alley in Manila with all her siblings, and the cousins they left behind.

Feedback from these students indicated that they appreciated the chance to work on something creative and personal—something special of their own that might never have been produced except for our little island of time together.

Fifth-Grade Biographies

After I had been working on this after-school project for a while, I realized that one of my colleagues was doing similar work with her class. Jocelyn Berke, my teacher book buddy, shares her fifth graders with my children two or three times a month. Each of my students has a fifth-grade buddy who chooses some special picture books to read aloud. My kids respond by reading something of their choice to their buddies. Everyone practices and everyone shares. I love the experience because the students all seem so thrilled to be working and sharing books with a child of another age level. Jocelyn and I watch, advise, and share literature and professional book recommendations with each other. Another side benefit for me is that I get to see what the fifth graders are doing.

Jocelyn loves teaching writing and had just completed a month-long biography unit with her fifth-grade class. She first shared many picture book biographies with students. She read them aloud and made them available to her fifth graders to read. Jocelyn gave several lessons about the craft behind the writing and spent about two weeks facilitating discussions. She helped her students study and analyze biographies and decide whether they wanted to write their pieces in a narrative style or produce a more factually based piece of writing. Jocelyn worked with her students in small groups to come up with four different areas of focus in the writing of biographies:

1. early life (interests, hobbies, education, important figures in the subjects' lives)
2. values (What was important to them, what were key motivations?)
3. important events (key steps that led them to become famous and successful in their fields)
4. actions (Why are they famous?)

As they learned about Frieda Kalho, Diego Rivera, Georgia O'Keefe, Jackie Robinson, and Neil Armstrong, among other notables, the fifth graders got a sense of what it means to live a life. As they read about people who lived great lives, they developed a feel for memoir. Their assignment was to a write a biography, written from personal knowledge of an adult in their family. Most of the fifth graders wrote about one of their parents. All the writing was done in the third person and was illustrated with varied media: colored pencil, pen, and crayon. Several included photographs. Jocelyn made sure to have a constant supply of biographies on hand so that students could sit with them and use them as models as they wrote their rough drafts. "I often referred students to other pieces of literature," Jocelyn said.

When their projects were finished, the students wrote reflections about what it had meant to them to write about someone in their families. Luis' reflection eloquently spoke of the importance of giving children these kinds of projects. (See Figure 9–1.)

These pieces of writing by the fifth graders were on display in our Martin School library and held a place of honor in South San Francisco's Orange Avenue Library as well, thanks to our librarian, Louella Angeles, who works in both places. South San Francisco Councilwoman Karyl Matsumoto was so impressed with the students' writing that she made a second trip to the public library to read each piece of work. "I can't begin to tell you how moved and impressed I was," she wrote to librarian Ann Mahon and to Jocelyn Berke. "What a wonderful project. Often times we go through life not aware of the sacrifices and the life experiences of our family members. In hindsight I wish I had sat down with my grandmother to learn of her experiences as an immigrant to the U.S."

Karyl Matsumoto spoke of these biographies at a South San Francisco City Council meeting and read one aloud.

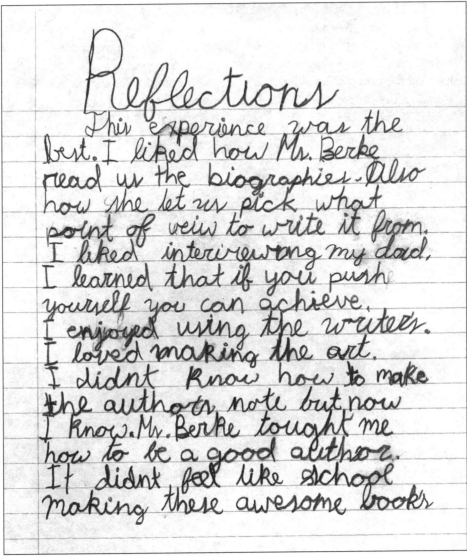

Reflections

This experience was the best. I liked how Mr. Berke read us the biographies. Also how she let us pick what point of veiw to write it from. I liked interviewing my dad. I learned that if you push yourself you can achieve. I enjoyed using the writers. I loved making the art. I didnt know how to make the authors note but now I know. Mr. Berke tought me how to be a good author. It didnt feel like school making these awesome books

Figure 9–1. Luis reflects on what it feels like to be an author.

I think we owe our students these kinds of moments and opportunities so they can spend some time on authentic learning of their own choosing. Renowned child psychiatrist Robert Coles spent his career investigating the inner lives of children through their words and their drawings. He believes that children from all over the world "disclose their convictions, feelings, and dreams with crayon, paint, and pencil" (1990). I believe this too. And I would add another way for children to express their deepest feelings and convictions: photography. I have seen my students grow in confidence, imagination, and critical thinking with cameras in their hands. Working to photograph and write about important people and experiences in their own lives gives children the resilience and strength to cope and to meet other challenges. As the poet William Carlos Williams said as he looked at children's drawings and scenes on paper, "Look at them looking. Their eyes meeting the world" (Coles 1992, 1).

References and Resources

References

Ackerman, Diane. 2000. *Deep Play*. New York: Knopf Publ. Jr.

Ada, Alma Flor. 2004. *I Love Saturdays y Domingos*. New York: Aladdin.

Alda, Arlene. 2002. *Arlene Alda's ABC: What Do You See?* Berkeley, CA: Tricycle.

———. 2004. *Arlene Alda's 1 2 3*. Berkeley, CA: Tricycle.

Ajmera, Maya, and John D. Ivanko. 1999. *To Be a Kid*. Watertown, MA: Charlesbridge.

Bull, Glen L., and Lynn Bell, eds. 2005. *Teaching with Digital Images: Acquire, Analyze, Create, Communicate*. Eugene, OR: International Society for Technology in Education.

Cole, Joanna. 1989. *The Magic School Bus: Inside the Earth*. New York: Scholastic.

Coles, Robert. 1990. *The Call of Stories: Teaching and the Moral Imagination. New Ed*. New York: Mariner Books.

———. 1992. *Their Eyes Meeting the World: The Drawings and Paintings of Children*. New York: Houghton Mifflin.

Collier, John Jr., Malcolm Collier, and Edward T. Hall. 1986. *Visual Anthropology: Photography as a Research Method*. Albuquerque: Univ. of New Mexico Press.

Condon, Mark W. F., and Michael McGuffee. 2001. *Real ePublishing, Really Publishing! How to Create Digital Books by and for All Ages*. Portsmouth, NH: Heinemann.

de Saint-Exupery, Antoine. 2003. *The Little Prince*. 60th anniv. ed. New York: Harcourt Children's Books.

Dorros, Arthur. 1997. *Abuela*. English ed. with Spanish phrases. New York: Picture Puffins.

Farrell, Catharine Horne. 1983. *Word Weaving: A Guide to Storytelling*. San Francisco: Zellerbach Family Fund.

Felleman, Hazel, and Edward Frank Allen. 1936. "The Reading Mother," in *Best Loved Poems of the American People*. New York: Doubleday.

Frasier, Debra. 2007. *Miss Alaineous: A Vocabulary Disaster*. New York: Voyager.

Freedman, Russell. 1990. *Children of the Wild West*. New York: Clarion.

———. 1998. *Kids at Work: Lewis Hine and the Crusade Against Child Labor*. New York: Clarion.

———. 2006. *Immigrant Kids*. New York: Scholastic.

Garza, Carmen Lomas. 1990. *Family Pictures/Cuadros de familia*. San Francisco: Children's Book Press.

———. 2000. *In My Family/En mí familia*. San Francisco: Children's Book Press.

———. 2003. *Magic Windows/Ventanas mágicas*. Bilingual ed. San Francisco: Children's Book Press.

Gherman, Beverly. 2002. *Ansel Adams: America's Photographer*. Boston: Little, Brown.

Haab, Sherri. 2002. *Making Mini-Books*. Palo Alto, CA: Klutz.

Halsman, Philippe. 1986. *Philippe Halsman's Jump Book*. New York: Harry N. Abrams.

Heacox, Kim. 2006. "Deadly Beauty: A Photographer Falls Under the Spell of Antarctica's Leopard Seals." Photographs by Paul Nicklen. *National Geographic* (November): pp. 68–91.

Irvine, Joan. 1988. *How to Make Pop-Ups*. New York: Morrow.

James, Ryan. 2004. *Photo Card Education Collection: Photos Included*. Budapest, Hungary: Ryan James.

Kalan, Robert. 1996. *Moving Day*. New York: Greenwillow.

Kennedy, John E. 2004. *Puppet Mania: The World's Most Incredible Puppet Making Book Ever*. Cincinnati: North Light.

Marzollo, Jean, and Walter Wick. 1995. *I Spy School Days: A Book of Picture Riddles*. I Spy Series. New York: Cartwheel Books.

McMillan, Bruce. 1982. *Puniddles*. New York: Houghton Mifflin.

———. 1992. *One Sun: A Book of Terse Verse*. New York: Holiday House.

———. 2001. *Puffins Climb, Penguins Rhyme*. New York: Voyager.

Mitchell, Lucy Sprague. 1951. *Our Children and Our Schools*. New York: Simon and Schuster.

Perez, Amanda Irma. 2002. *My Diary from Here to There/Mi diario de aquí hasta allá*. San Francisco: Children's Book Press.

Petrich, Patricia, and Rosemary Dalton. 1975. *The Kid's Arts and Crafts Book*. Concord, CA: Nitty Gritty.

Raffi. 1996. *Spider on the Floor*. Songs to Read Series. New York: Crown.

Regan, Margaret, comp. 2000. *Our Peaceable Kingdom: The Photographs of John Drysdale*. New York: St. Martin's.

Routman, Regie. 2000. *Kids' Poems: Teaching First Graders to Love Writing Poetry*. Kids' Poems Series. New York: Scholastic.

Smith, Frank. 1986. *Insult to Intelligence: The Bureaucratic Invasion of Our Classrooms*. New York: Arbor House.

Tucker, Jean S. 1994. *Come Look with Me: Discovering Photographs with Children*. Charlottesville, VA: Thomasson-Grant.

Vygotsky, Lev S. 1986. *Thought and Language*. Rev. ed. Cambridge, MA: MIT Press.

Weed, Paula, and Carla Jimison. 2001. *Tricky Pix: Do It Yourself Trick Photography*. (Comes with camera). Palo Alto, CA: Klutz.

Wiesner, David. 2001. *The Three Pigs*. New York: Clarion.

———. 2006. *Flotsam*. New York: Clarion.

Wildsmith, Brian. 1997. *Brian Wildsmith's Amazing World of Words*. Brookfield, CT: Millbrook.

Wood, Audrey. 2000. *The Flying Dragon Room*. New York: Scholastic.

Wyndham, Robert. 1998. *Chinese Mother Goose Rhymes*. New York: Putnam Juvenile.

Yolen, Jane. 2003. *How Does a Dinosaur Say Good Night?* New York: Picture Lions.

———. 2006. *How Do Dinosaurs Play with Their Friends?* Board book ed. White Plains, NY: Blue Sky.

Additional Resources

Books for Stimulating Creativity: Photography, Art, Writing (a Small Sampling)

Brown, Anthony. 2001. *Voices in the Park*. New York: DK Children.

Carter, David A. 2007. *Black Spots: A Pop-Up Book for Children of All Ages*. New York: Little Simon.

King, B. A., and Tomie dePaola. 1979. *Criss-Cross, Applesauce*. York, PA: Matrix.

McLerran, Alice. 1992. *Roxaboxen*. New York: Pearson.

Schotter, Roni. 1999. *Nothing Ever Happens on 90th Street*. New York: Scholastic.

Children's Books Featuring Art

Anholt, Laurence. 2003. *The Magical Garden of Claude Monet*. New York: Barron's Educational Series.

Bjork, Cristina. 1987. *Linnea in Monet's Garden*. New York: R and S.

Mayhew, James. 2004. *Katie's Picture Show*. New York: Orchard Books.

McClintock, Barbara. 2006. *Adele and Simon*. New York: Farrar, Straus, and Giroux.

Winter, Jeanette. 2003. *My Name Is Georgia: A Portrait by Jeanette Winter*. New York: Voyager.

Winter, Jonah. 2007. *Diego*. New York: Knopf.

Winter, Jonah, and Ana Juan. 2002. *Frida*. New York: Arthur A. Levine Books.

Children's Books Featuring Photography

Martin, Jacqueline Briggs. 1998. *Snowflake Bentley*. Boston: Houghton Mifflin.

Willard, Nancy. 1994. *Simple Pictures Are Best*. New York: Scholastic.

Children's Books for Developing Vocabulary and Language

Banks, Kate. 2006. *Max's Words*. New York: Random House.

Burningham, John. 2002. *Would You Rather?* Zurich, Switzerland: North-South/Sea-Star.

Fleming, Denise. 2002. *Alphabet Under Construction.* New York: Holt.

Johnson, Stephen T. 1995. *Alphabet City.* New York: Puffin.

Reinhart, Matthew. 2002. *Animal Popposites: A Pop-Up Book of Opposites.* New York: Little Simon.

Children's Books to Stimulate Storytelling and Memoir

Ada, Alma Flor. 1995. *My Name Is María Isabel.* New York: Aladdin.

Aliki. 1998. *Marianthe's Story: Painted Words/Spoken Memories.* New York: Greenwillow.

Banyai, Istvan. 1998. *Zoom.* New York: Picture Puffin.

———. 2000. *Re-zoom.* New York: Picture Puffin.

Bradby, Marie. 1995. *More Than Anything Else.* New York: Scholastic.

Bunting, Eve. 1993. *Fly Away Home.* New York: Clarion.

Cooney, Barbara. 1982. *Miss Rumphius.* New York: Penguin Putnam.

dePaola, Tomie. 2000. *Nana Upstairs and Nana Downstairs.* New York: Putnam Juvenile.

Fox, Mem. 1989. *Wilfred Gordon McDonald Partridge.* La Jolla, CA: Kane/Miller.

Hearne, Betsy. 1997. *Seven Brave Women.* New York: Greenwillow.

Houston, Gloria. 1992. *My Great-Aunt Arizona.* New York: HarperCollins.

Lamorisse, Albert. 1967. *The Red Balloon.* New York: Doubleday.

Lehman, Barbara. 2004. *The Red Book.* Boston: Houghton Mifflin.

Mitchell, Margaree K. 1998. *Uncle Jed's Barbershop.* New York: Aladdin.

Murphy, Frank. 2005. *Babe Ruth Saves Baseball.* New York: Random House.

Ringgold, Faith. 1991. *Tar Beach.* New York: Crown.

Rylant, Cynthia. 1992. *When I Was Young in the Mountains.* New York: Dutton.

Soto, Gary. 1993. *Too Many Tamales.* New York: Putnam.

Steig, William. 1999. *Sylvester and the Magic Pebble.* New York: Aladdin.

Wells, Rosemary. 1992. *Voyage to the Bunny Planet: First Tomato, Moss Pillows, Island Light.* Boxed set. New York: Dial.

Yashima, Taro. 1976. *Crow Boy.* New York: Viking.

Children's Books with Photographic Illustrations (a Small Sampling)

Cooper, Michael L. 2004. *Dust to Eat: Drought and Depression in the 1930's.* New York: Clarion.

Hoban, Tana. 1990. *Shadows and Reflections.* New York: Greenwillow.

———. 1995. *26 Letters and 99 Cents.* New York: HarperTrophy.

———. 1997. *Exactly the Opposite.* New York: Harper Trophy.

Kindersley, Annabelle, and Barnabas Kindersley. 1995. *Children Just Like Me.* New York: DK Children.

———. 1997a. *Celebrations: Festivals, Carnivals, and Feast Days from Around the World.* Collingdale, PA: DK Children.

————. 1997b. *Children Just Like Me: Celebrations!* New York: DK Children.

Schwartz, David, and Yael Schy. 2007. *Where in the Wild? Camouflaged Creatures Concealed . . . and Revealed.* Photographs by Dwight Kuhn. Berkeley, CA: Tricycle.

Craft Book for Children and Adults

Carle, Eric. 1998. *You Can Make a Collage: A Very Simple How-to Book.* Palo Alto, CA: Klutz.

Magazines

Book Links: Connecting Books, Libraries, and Classrooms. Published six times a year by Booklist Publications, PO Box 615, Mt. Morris, IL, 65054-7564.

The Horn Book Guide to Children's and Young Adult Books. Published twice a year by the Horn Book, Inc., 56 Roland Street, Suite 200, Boston, MA, 02129.

The Horn Book Magazine. Published six times a year by the Horn Book, Inc., 56 Roland Street, Suite 200, Boston, MA, 02129.

School Library Journal. Published twelve times a year by Cahners Business Information, 245 West Seventeenth Street, New York, NY, 10011.

Magazines for Children

Highlights for Children. Online: www.highlights.com.

National Geographic World. National Geographic Society, Washington, DC, 20036.

Ranger Rick. National Wildlife Association, 8925 Leesburg Pike, Vienna, VA, 22184. Online: www.nwf.org.

Zoobooks. Wildlife Education Ltd., 12233 Thatcher Court, Poway, CA, 92064-5880. Online: www.zoobooks.com.

Photography How-to Books for Children

Bidner, Jenni. 2004. *The Kids' Guide to Digital Photography: How to Shoot, Save, Play with and Print Your Digital Photos.* Asheville, NC: Lark Books.

Friedman, Debra. 2003. *Picture This: Fun Photography and Crafts.* Toronto, Ontario: Kids Can.

Poetry for Children

deRegniers, Beatrice Shenk. 1988. *Sing a Song of Popcorn: Every Child's Book of Poems.* Reprint. New York: Scholastic.

Johnston, Tony. 1996. *My Mexico/México mío.* (Poetry in English and Spanish). New York: Penguin Putnam.

Prelutsky, Jack, and Christine Davinier. 2007. *Me I Am!* New York: Farrar, Straus and Giroux.

Prelutsky, Jack, and Arnold Lobel. 1983. *The Random House Book of Poetry for Children.* New York: Random House.

Yolen, Jane, and Andrew Fusek Peters, comps. 2007. *Here's a Little Poem: A Very First Book of Poetry.* Cambridge, MA: Candlewick.

Professional Development Resources

Almy, Millie Corinne, and Celia Genishi. 1979. *Ways of Studying Children: An Observation Manual for Early Childhood Teachers.* Williston, VT: Teachers College Press.

Briski, Zana, Ross Kauffman, John McDowell, and Nancy Baker. 2005. *Born into Brothels.* DVD. New York: HBO/Cinemax Documentary Films. (For more information, contact Kids with Cameras, www.kids-with-cameras.org.)

Briski, Zana, and Kids with Cameras. 2004. *Born into Brothels: Photographs by the Children of Calcutta.* New York: Umbrage Editions.

Brookman, Philip. 1991. *Shooting Back: Photography by and About the Homeless.* Washington, DC: Washington Project for the Arts.

Cary, Stephen. 2007. *Working with Second Language Learners: Answers to Teachers' Top Ten Questions.* 2d ed. Portsmouth, NH: Heinemann.

Dragan, Pat Barrett. 2001. *Literacy from Day One.* Portsmouth, NH: Heinemann.

———. 2003. *Everything You Need to Know to Teach First Grade.* Portsmouth, NH: Heinemann.

———. 2005. *The How-to Guide for Teaching English Language Learners in the Primary Classroom.* Portsmouth, NH: Heinemann.

Entz, Susan, and Lyn Galarza. 2000. *Picture This: Digital and Instant Photography Activities for Early Childhood Learning.* Thousand Oaks, CA: Corwin.

Ernst, Karen. 1994. *Picturing Learning: Artists and Writers in the Classroom.* Portsmouth, NH: Heinemann.

Ewald, Wendy, and Alexandra Lightfoot. 2001. *I Wanna Take Me a Picture: Teaching Photography and Writing to Children.* Boston: Beacon.

Harrison, Holly. 2003. *Altered Books, Collaborative Journals, and Other Adventures in Bookmaking.* Beverly, MA: Quarry Books.

Rand, Glenn, and Richard Zakia. 2006. *Teaching Photography: Tools for the Imaging Educator.* Burlington, MA: Focal.

Van Gorp, Lynn. 2001. *Digital Photography in the Classroom: Grades 4 and Up.* Westminster, CA: Teacher Created Resources.

References and Books About Photographers

Partridge, Elizabeth. 2002. *Restless Spirit: The Life and Work of Dorthea Lange.* New York: Scholastic.

Sandler, Martin W. 2005. *America Through the Lens: Photographers Who Changed the Nation.* New York: Henry Holt.

Riddles and Rhymes for Children

Cerf, Bennett. 1999. *Riddles and More Riddles.* New York: Random House.

Cole, Joanna, and Stephanie Calmenson, comps. 1994. *Why Did the Chicken Cross the Road? And Other Riddles, Old and New.* New York: Morrow Junior Books.

Dahl, Michael. 2003. *Animal Quack-Ups.* Mankato, MN: Picture Window Books.

Hall, Katy, and Lisa Eisenberg. 2005. *Stinky Riddles.* New York: Dial.

Rosenbloom, Joseph. 1976. *The Biggest Riddle Book in the World.* New York: Sterling.

Websites

CameraScope, available for free download: www.teacherlink.org/tools (see Chapter 5)

National Gallery of Art Classroom: www.nga.gov/education/classroom/index.htm (Digital images and teaching resources for K–12 teachers. Main website for teachers who are working to integrate the arts into curriculum. It includes lessons for teachers and interactive experiences for students. Resources are listed by curriculum topic, art subject, or the artist's name.)

NGA Kids: www.nga.gov/kids/kids.htm

RealeBooks publishing site: www.realebooks.com

Shutterfly: Classroom Creativity with Scholastic: www.shutterfly.com/info/acquisition/scholasticschool.jsp

Art Prints

National Gallery of Art: www.nga.gov

Shorewood Educational: www.artforschools.com

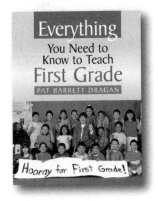
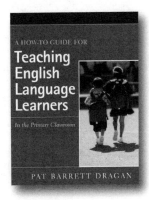